Amber Valley

The heart of Derbyshire

Amber Valley is one of the largest Boroughs in Derbyshire with a population of around 116,000. The main centres of population are based around the thriving market towns of Alfreton, Belper, Heanor and Ripley.

The geographic area comprises of Dethick, Lea and Holloway in the north to Mackworth and Kirk Langley in the south. The Parish of Turnditch is to the west of the Borough whilst the county border with Nottinghamshire forms the eastern boundary. The area has a great deal of scenic beauty, situated on the southern tip of the Pennine Chain and there are many attractive and interesting villages.

Historically, the towns and settlements along the eastern side of the Borough developed with the growth in iron, coal and clay industries. On the western side, the power of the River Derwent was harnessed by industrialists for their textile mills and the area became known as the Cradle of the Industrial Revolution. This strong manufacturing base has developed over the years and there is now a network of factory shop outlets including the world famous Denby Pottery Visitor Centre. The area has also always had a strong agricultural base. This varied commercial background has meant that there is a skilled local workforce which combined with excellent transport links has brought many new organisations to Amber Valley.

Nowadays, visitors are drawn to the area because of the diverse range of attractions which include Kedleston Hall and Wingfield Manor. The National Tramway Museum and Midland Railway Centre are both based in Amber Valley, whilst in complete contrast the American Adventure Theme Park is situated next to Shipley Country Park. There are also beautiful gardens at Lea, or enjoy outdoor summer concerts at Belper River Gardens. The River Derwent is the link in the chain that forms the National Heritage Corridor™ and the Derwent Valley Visitor Centre is situated at Belper.

Each of the towns has a modern Leisure Centre with swimming pools and opportunities for varied sporting activities. There are also public libraries and heritage centres in every town. The Town Centre Bureaux will help with information on Council Services and Amber Valley's Tourist Information Centre is located at Ripley.

There is a range of housing available from new developments to property in conservation areas. Details on the various schools and colleges which serve the Borough may be obtained from the local Education Office. There is also a well established community education programme which operates throughout the area.

Whilst every effort has been made to ensure the accuracy of the information contained in this guide, neither the publishers, Gray Associates, nor Amber Valley Borough Council, can be held responsible for any errors or omissions (March 1999).

Borough Development, Amber Valley Borough Council,
Town Hall, Market Place, Ripley,
Derbyshire DE5 3BT

Printed by Slater Printing Limited.

Amber Valley

Useful Information

Allotments

For details about allotments in the Borough
Tel:01773 841412

Amber Valley Borough Council

(for all Departments)
Town Hall,
Market Place,
Ripley,
Derbyshire DE5 3XE
Tel:01773 570222
Fax:01773 841616
Minicom: 01773 841490
E.Mail: enquiry@ambervalley.gov.uk
Website: http://www.ambervalley.gov.uk

Amber Valley Town Centre Bureaux

(for payment and enquiries)
Alfreton House,
High Street,
Alfreton,
Derbyshire DE55 7HH

King Street,
Belper,
Derbyshire DE56 1PX

Town Hall,
Market Place,
Heanor,
Derbyshire DE75 7EG

Town Hall,
Market Place,
Ripley,
Derbyshire DE5 3WZ

Area

26,512 hectares(65,577 acres)

Attractions

Alfreton District Heritage Trust

Heritage Centre,
Rodgers Lane,
Alfreton,
Derbyshire DE55 7FF
Tel:01773 831682

American Adventure

Ilkeston,
Derbyshire
DE7 5SX
Tel:01773 531521
Fax:01773 716140

Belper Heritage Centre

St John's Chapel,
The Butts,
Belper,
Derbyshire DE56 1HX
Tel: 01773 822116

Belper River Gardens

Boat Trips
Tel:01773 841415

Canals and Waterways

Tel:01159 461017

Carnfield Hall

South Normanton,
Derbyshire DE55 2BE
Tel:01773 520084

Denby Pottery Visitor Centre

Denby,
Ripley,
Derbyshire DE5 8NX
Tel:01773 740799
Fax:01773 740749

Derwent Valley Visitor Centre

North Mill,
Bridgefoot,
Belper,
Derbyshire DE56 1YD
Tel:01773 880474

Dolls House Emporium

Victoria Road,
Ripley,
Derbyshire DE5 3YD
Tel:01773 513773

Great Northern Basin

Langley Mill,
Derbyshire
Tel:0115 9328042

Heage Windmill

Dungeley Hill,
Nether Heage,
Derbyshire
Tel: 01773 856467

Heanor Heritage Centre

Marlpool Cemetery Chapel,
Ilkeston Road, (main entrance),
Lockton Avenue,
Heanor,
Derbyshire
Tel: 01773 768174

Kedleston Hall

Kedleston,

Derbyshire DE22 5JH

Tel:01332 842191

Fax:01332 841972

Lea Gardens

Lea,

Derbyshire DE4 5GH

Tel:01629 534380

Fax:01629 534260

Midland Railway Centre

Butterley Station,

Ripley,

Derbyshire DE5 3QZ

Tel:01773 747674

Fax:01773 570721

National Tramway Museum

Crich,

Matlock,

Derbyshire DE4 5DP

Tel:01773 852565

Fax:01773 852326

Ripley Heritage Centre

33 Market Place,

Ripley,

Derbyshire

Tel:01773 513189

The Sherwood Foresters War Memorial

Crich,

Matlock,

Derbyshire

Tel:01773 852350

Tel:0115 9465415

Shipley Country Park

Visitor Centre,

Slack Lane,

Heanor,

Derbyshire DE75 7GX

Tel:01773 719961

Fax:01773 715023

Wingfield Manor

South Wingfield,

Alfreton,

Derbyshire DE55 7GX

Tel:01773 832060

Benefits Agency

Forester House,
Becket Street,
Derby DE1 1NW
Tel: 01332 243800

St Andrews House,
201 London Road,
Derby DE1 2TZ
Tel:01332 254200

58 South Street,
Ilkeston,
Derbyshire DE72 8TU
Tel:0115 9448000

Business Link

PO Box 18,
Town Hall,
Ripley,
Derbyshire DE5 3SZ
Tel:01773 841384
Fax:01773 841523

Citizens Advice Bureau

Progressive Building,
Sitwell Street,·
Derby DE1 2JT
Tel:01332 243120 (general)
Tel:01332 366548 (financial)
Fax:01332 291310

Combined Courts

Morledge,
Derby
Tel:01332 622600
Fax:01332 622543

Community Transport

2 Long Close,
Cemetery Lane,
Ripley,
Derbyshire DE5 3HY
Tel:01773 746652

Council for Voluntary Service

33 Market Place,
Ripley,
Derbyshire DE5 3HA
Tel:01773 512076

County Council

County Hall,
Matlock,
Derbyshire DE4 3AG
Tel: 01629 580000
Fax: 01629 585121

Derbyshire Careers Services Centre

Market House,
Market Place,
Ripley,
Derbyshire DE5 3BR
Tel:01773 745921

Derbyshire Tourist Guides

Bookings Officer,
Holloway House,
Holloway,
Nr Matlock,
Derbyshire DE4 5AT
Tel:01629 534284

Disabled People

Derbyshire Centre for Integrated Living,
Long Close,
Ripley,
Derbyshire DE5 3HY
Tel:01773 740246
Fax:01773 570185
Minicom:01773 748452

Early Closing Day

Wednesday throughout the Borough

Education

Area Office,
Grosvenor Road,
Ripley,
Derbyshire DE5 3JE
Tel:01773 744741

Electricity

Emergencies
Tel:0345 080080
Customer Services
Tel:0345 363363

Events

For up to date information contact the
Tourist Information Centre at Ripley
Tel:01773 841488
Fax: 01773 841487

Fire

Stations: Alfreton, Belper, Crich, Duffield,
Heanor and Ripley
Headquarters:
Old Hall,
Burton Road,
Littleover,
Derby DE23 6EH
Tel:01332 771221
NB In case of fire, ring 999

Gas

Billing
Tel:0645 555400

Service & Repair Enquiries
Tel:0645 605040
Tel:0645 500400

Emergency - Call Free
Tel:0800 111999

Highways

Main Roads -
Derbyshire County Council,
Derby Road,
Duffield,
Derbyshire DE56 4FN
Tel:01332 842244

Other Roads -
Amber Valley Borough Council
Town Hall,
Ripley,
Derbyshire DE5 3XE
Tel:01773 570222

Hospitals

Babington Hospital
Derby Road,
Belper,
Derbyshire DE56 1WH
Tel:01773 824171

Derby City & Children's Hospital
Uttoxeter Road,
Derby DE22 3NE
Tel:01332 340131

Derbyshire Royal Infirmary
London Road,
Derby DE1 2QY
Tel:01332 347141

Heanor Memorial Hospital
Ilkeston Road,
Heanor,
Derbyshire DE75 7EA
Tel:01773 710711

Ilkeston Community/General
Heanor Road,
Ilkeston,
Derbyshire DE7 8LN
Tel:0115 9305522

Ripley Hospital
Sandham Lane,
Ripley,
Derbyshire DE5 3HE
Tel:01773 743456

(Casualties are dealt with at the Derbyshire
Royal Infirmary ONLY)

Inland Revenue

Horsefair House,
35 King Street,
Alfreton,
Derbyshire DE55 7BG
Tel:01773 523100

Northgate House,
Agard Street,
Derby DE1 1RU
Tel:01332 724000

Job Centres

Marshall Street,
Alfreton,
Derbyshire DE55 7BX
Tel:01773 724700

54 King Street,
Belper,
Derbyshire DE56 1PN
Tel:01773 723000

Howitt Buildings,
High Street,
Heanor,
Derbyshire DE75 7EZ
Tel:01773 723200

Leisure/Sports Facilities

Alfreton Leisure Centre,
Church Street,
Alfreton,
Derbyshire DE55 7BD
Tel:01773 834817

Belper Sports Centre,
Kilbourne Road,
Belper,
Derbyshire DE56 1RZ
Tel:01773 825285

Charles Hill Sports Hall,
Flamstead Avenue,
Loscoe,
Heanor,
Derbyshire DE75 7RN
Tel:01773 761551

Heanor Leisure Centre,
Hands Road,
Heanor,
Derbyshire DE75 7HA
Tel:01773 769711

Ripley Leisure Centre,
Derby Road,
Ripley,
Derbyshire DE5 3HR
Tel:01773 746531

All Centres have excellent catering facilities
and are used for concerts, exhibitions, etc.
Outdoor football, hockey and cricket
pitches, bookings by Amber Valley Borough
Council.
Tel:01773 570222 Ext. 2411.

Libraries

Severn Square,
Alfreton,
Derbyshire DE55 7BQ
Tel:01773 833199

Bridge Street,
Belper,
Derbyshire DE56 1BA
Tel:01773 824333

Wirksworth Road,
Duffield,
Derbyshire DE56 4GH
Tel:01332 840324

Ilkeston Road,
Heanor,
Derbyshire DE75 7DX
Tel:01773 712482
Fax:01773 535465

Grosvenor Road,
Ripley,
Derbyshire DE5 3JE
Tel:01773 743321
Fax:01773 741057

Bank Street,
Somercotes,
Derbyshire DE55 4JE (part time)
Tel:01773 540514

All other areas in the Borough are visited
by the Mobile Library. Details of the
timetable may be obtained from Belper
Library.

Magistrates Court

The Court House,
Pimlico,
Ilkeston,
Derbyshire DE7 5HZ
Tel:0115 9320286

Markets

Alfreton - Tuesday, Thursday, Friday and
Saturday (indoor)
Belper - Saturday (outdoor)
Heanor - Friday and Saturday (outdoor)
Ripley - Friday and Saturday (outdoor)

National Express

Bookings may be made at the Tourist
Information Centre, Ripley.
Tel:01773 841488
Fax:01773 841487

Newspapers

Daily
Derby Evening Telegraph,
Northcliffe House,
Meadow Road,
Derby DE1 2DW
Tel:01332 291111

Nottingham Evening Post Group Limited,
Castle Wharf House,
Nottingham NG1 7EU
Tel:0115 9482000

Weekly
Belper News,
8 Market Place,
Belper,
Derbyshire DE56 1FZ
Tel:01773 820939

Derbyshire Times,
98 High Street,
Alfreton,
Derbyshire DE55 7BE
Tel:01773 834731

Ripley & Heanor News,
27 Grosvenor Road,
Ripley,
Derbyshire DE5 3JE
Tel:01773 742133

Free
Express Newspapers,
Northcliffe House,
Meadow Road,
Derby DE1 2DW
Tel:01332 292222

The Trader Group of Newspapers,
52 Babington Lane,
Derby DE1 1SX
Tel:01332 253999

The District of Amber Valley comprises the following parishes:
Aldercar & Langley Mill, Alderwasley, Alfreton, Ashleyhay, Belper, Codnor, Crich, Denby, Dethick, Lea & Holloway, Duffield, Hazelwood, Heanor & Loscoe, Holbrook, Horsley, Horsley Woodhouse, Idridgehay & Alton, Ironville, Kedleston, Kilburn, Kirk Langley, Mackworth, Mapperley, Pentrich, Quarndon, Ravensdale Park, Ripley, Shipley, Shottle & Postern, Smalley, Somercotes, South Wingfield, Swanwick, Turnditch, Weston Underwood, Windley. Riddings is the only unparished area in the Borough.

Amber Valley Constituency - Comprises

(a)
Borough of Amber Valley:
Aldercar, Alfreton East, Alfreton West, Codnor, Crich, Denby and Horsley Woodhouse, Heage and Ambergate, Heanor and Loscoe, Heanor East, Heanor West, Holbrook and Horsley, Kilburn, Riddings, Ripley, Ripley and Marehay, Shipley Park, Somercotes, Swanwick, Wingfield.

(b)
Borough of Erewash:
Breadsall, Little Eaton, Morley and Stanley.

Member: Judy Mallaber - Labour
House of Commons
London SW1A 0AA
(All correspondence to this address)
Tel: 0171 2193428
Fax: 0171 2190991

Constituency Office:
Prospect House,
Nottingham Road,
Ripley,
Derbyshire DE5 3AZ
Tel: 01773 512792
Fax: 01773 742393

West Derbyshire Constituency - Comprises

(a)
Borough of Amber Valley
Alport, Belper East, Belper North, Belper South, Duffield, South West Parishes.

(b)
District of Derbyshire Dales - Whole District.

Member: Patrick Allan McLoughlin - Conservative
House of Commons,
London SW1A 0AA
(All correspondence to this address)
Tel:0171 2194058
Fax:0171 2194871

Constituency Office:
3 Rutland Street,
Matlock,
Derbyshire DE4 3GM
Tel:01629 57205
Fax:01629 580943

European Parliament
(Peak District Constituency)
Member: Arlene McCarthy - Labour
Talbot House,
Talbot Road,
Glossop,
Derbyshire SK13 7DP
Tel:01457 857300
Fax:01457 867339

Sub office: 23 Barratt Lane
Attenborough
Notts NG9 6AG
Tel:0115 9259716

Police

Headquarters,
Butterley Hall,
Ripley,
Derbyshire DE5 3RS
Tel:01773 570100
Fax:01773 572225

Police Stations (opening hours vary)

Hall Street,
Alfreton
Derbyshire DE55 7BS
Tel:01773 830000
Fax:01773 522003

Field Lane,
Belper,
Derbyshire DE56 100
Tel:01773 823821
Fax:01773 522059

Wilmot Street,
Heanor,
Derbyshire DE75 7EH
Tel:01773 530101
Fax:01773 522234

Moseley Street,
Ripley,
Derbyshire DE5 3DA
Tel:01773 570101
Fax:01773 522060

Population

Alfreton (including Riddings, Somercotes	
& Swanwick)	25040
Belper	19420
Heanor & Loscoe	17050
Ripley & Marehay	15020
Rest of Amber Valley	39670
Total population	116,200

Post Offices

Main Offices
Institute Lane,
Alfreton,
Derbyshire DE55 7AA
Tel: 01773 832072

Strutt Street,
Belper,
Derbyshire DE56 1UN
Tel: 01773 820108

14 Godfrey Street,
Heanor,
Derbyshire DE75 7GD
Tel:01773 713034

Derby Road,
Ripley,
Derbyshire DE5 3YA
Tel:01773 512932

There are Sub Post Offices throughout the
Borough.

Probation Service

1 Institute Lane, Alfreton,
Derbyshire DE55 7BQ
Tel:01773 833074
Fax:01773 831944

2 Siddals Road, Derby
DE1 2PB
Tel:01332 340047
Fax:01332 340056

34 South Street, Ilkeston,
Derbyshire DE7 5QE
Tel:0115 9301123
Fax:0115 9302503

Radio Stations

Radio Derby
St Helens Street,
Derbyshire DE1 3HY
Tel: 01332 361111
Fax:01332 290794

Ram FM
Tel:01332 292945

Registrar

Town Centre Bureau,
King Street,
Belper,
Derbyshire DE56 1PX
Thursday 9.30 am - 12.00 noon

87 Lord Haddon Road,
Ilkeston,
Derbyshire DE7 8AX
Tel:0115 9324844/9321014
Fax:0115 9326450
Mon - Fri
9.30 am - 12.30 pm; 2.00 pm - 4.30 pm
Sat - by appointment only.

Town Hall,
Market Place,
Ripley,
Derbyshire
Tel:01773 841380/841381
Monday - Friday
9.15 am - 12.45 pm; 1.30 pm - 4.00 pm

Rent Officer

10 De Bradelie House,
Chapel Street,
Belper,
Derbyshire DE56 1YF
Tel:01773 822992
Fax:01773 823854

Social Services

Amber Valley Area Office,
Cemetery Lane,
Ripley,
Derbyshire DE5 3HY
Tel:01773 728000
Fax:01773 728111

South East Derbyshire College

Field Road,
Ilkeston,
Derbyshire DE7 5RS
Tel:01159 324212
Fax:01159 326735

Telephone Service

Retail Enquiries
24/28 St Peter's Churchyard
Derby
Tel: 0800 800150

Theatres

For local and London theatre bookings,
contact the Tourist Information Centre,
Ripley
Tel: 01773 841488

Trading Standards

Head Office,
Chatsworth Hall,
Chesterfield Road,
Matlock,
Derbyshire DE4 3AG
Tel:01629 580000

Tourist Information Centre

Market Place,
Ripley,
Derbyshire DE5 3BT
Tel:01773 841488
Fax:01773 841487
Email: tourism@ambervalley.gov.uk
Website: http://www.ambervalley.gov.uk

Transport

By road -
From the north and south, the M1 runs
parallel to the eastern boundary with
access at junctions 26 and 28. The A6
gives access to major trunk roads via the
A52 and the Borough is crossed by the
A38.

By rail -
There are stations at Alfreton, Ambergate,
Belper, Duffield, Langley Mill and
Whatstandwell.
For information Tel:0345 484950

By coach-
For up to date information on local services
Tel:01332 292200
(7.00 am - 8.00 pm)

By air -
East Midlands International Airport
Tel:01332 852852
Birmingham International Airport
Tel:0121 7675511
Manchester International Airport
Tel:0161 4893000

By sea -
Hull - North Sea Ferries Tel:01482 377177
Harwich - Stena Line Tel:01255 243333

Eurotunnel
Tel:0990 353535

Twinned Towns

Amber Valley is twinned with the
Blackstone Valley, Rhode Island, USA.
Belper is twinned with Pawtucket, Rhode
Island, USA.
Ripley is twinned with Chateau Renault,
France.

Water

Derby District,
Raynesway,
Derby DE21 7JA
Tel:01332 669966

Key to map symbols

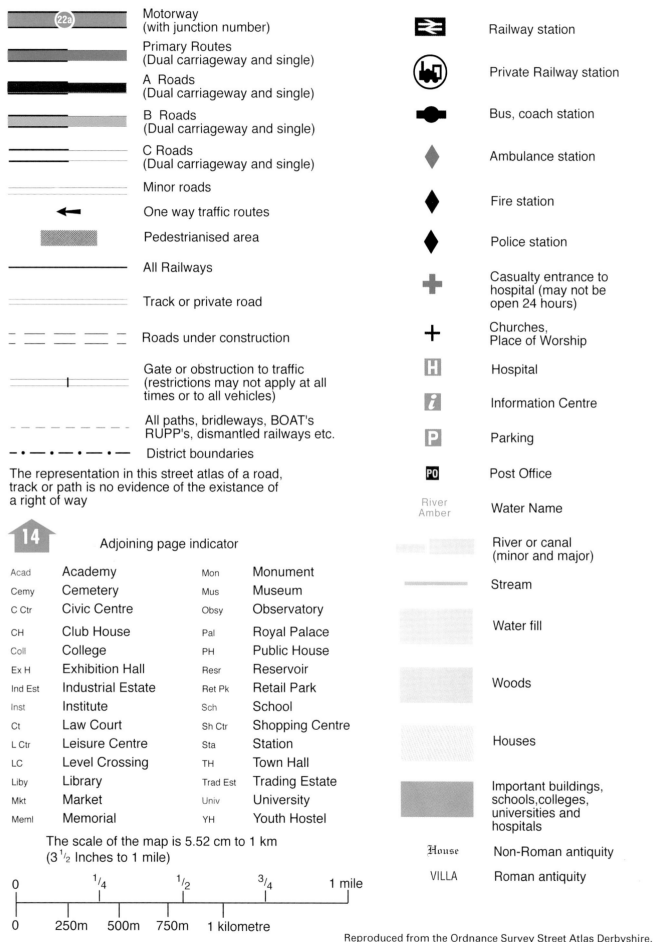

Motorway
(with junction number)

Primary Routes
(Dual carriageway and single)

A Roads
(Dual carriageway and single)

B Roads
(Dual carriageway and single)

C Roads
(Dual carriageway and single)

Minor roads

One way traffic routes

Pedestrianised area

All Railways

Track or private road

Roads under construction

Gate or obstruction to traffic
(restrictions may not apply at all
times or to all vehicles)

All paths, bridleways, BOAT's
RUPP's, dismantled railways etc.

District boundaries

The representation in this street atlas of a road,
track or path is no evidence of the existance of
a right of way

14 Adjoining page indicator

Acad	Academy	Mon	Monument
Cemy	Cemetery	Mus	Museum
C Ctr	Civic Centre	Obsy	Observatory
CH	Club House	Pal	Royal Palace
Coll	College	PH	Public House
Ex H	Exhibition Hall	Resr	Reservoir
Ind Est	Industrial Estate	Ret Pk	Retail Park
Inst	Institute	Sch	School
Ct	Law Court	Sh Ctr	Shopping Centre
L Ctr	Leisure Centre	Sta	Station
LC	Level Crossing	TH	Town Hall
Liby	Library	Trad Est	Trading Estate
Mkt	Market	Univ	University
Meml	Memorial	YH	Youth Hostel

The scale of the map is 5.52 cm to 1 km
(3 ½ Inches to 1 mile)

0   ¼   ½   ¾   1 mile

0   250m   500m   750m   1 kilometre

Railway station

Private Railway station

Bus, coach station

Ambulance station

Fire station

Police station

Casualty entrance to
hospital (may not be
open 24 hours)

Churches,
Place of Worship

Hospital

Information Centre

Parking

Post Office

River
Amber   Water Name

River or canal
(minor and major)

Stream

Water fill

Woods

Houses

Important buildings,
schools,colleges,
universities and
hospitals

House   Non-Roman antiquity

VILLA   Roman antiquity

Alfreton Gazetteer

Abbott Rd. Alf DE55 .... B2
Addison Dr. Alf DE55 .... B2
Alfred St. Alf DE55 .... A2
Alfreton L Ctr. Alf DE55 .... A2
Alfreton Rd Alf DE55 .... B4
Alfreton Sta. Alf DE55 ...... C3
Alfreton Trad Est. Alf DE55 ...
.... B1
Alma St. Alf DE55 .... B2
Amber Gr. Alf DE55 .... A1
Arthur St. Alf DE55 .... B3
Ashfield Ave. Som DE55 .. C1

Beech Ave. Alf DE55 .... B3
Beechdale Rd. Alf DE55 ... C2
Belvoir Way. Som DE55 ... C1
Bentley Cl. Alf DE55 .... B2
Birch Cl. Alf DE55 .... B3
Birchwood Rd. Alf DE55 ... C2
Birchwood Way. Som ....
DE55 .... C1
Bishop St. Alf DE55 .... B3
Bonsall La. Alf DE55 .... A2
Briar Cl. Alf DE55 .... C2
Brook Ave. Alf DE55 .... B2
Brook Cl. Alf DE55 .... B2
Brook La. Alf DE55 .... B2
Byron Ave. Alf DE55 .... B2

Carnfield Hall. S Norm ....
DE55 .... C3
Carnfield Hill. S Norm ....
DE55 .... C3
Catherine St. Alf DE55 ..... C2
Cedar Ave. Alf DE55 .... B3
Central Rd. Alf DE55 .... B2
Chapel St. Alf DE55 .... B2
Charles St. Alf DE55 .... B3
Chatham Ave. Alf DE55 .... C2
Chatsworth Cl. Alf DE55 ... A2
Chesterfield Rd. Alf DE55 A3
Christ the King RC Prim Sch.
Alf DE55 .... B3
Church St. Alf DE55 .... A2
Colin St. Alf DE55 .... B2
Colliery Row. Alf DE55 ..... B3
Connaught Ct. Alf DE55 .... B2

Copthorne Inf Sch. Alf ....
DE55 .... B3
Cornhill Ct. Alf DE55 .... B2
Cornhill Dr. Alf DE55 .... B2
Cotes Park Ind Est. Alf ....
DE55 .... C1
Cotes Park La. Som DE55 C1
Coupland Pl. Som DE55 ... C1
Cowham Cl. Alf DE55 .... C2
Crescent The. Alf DE55 .... B2
Cressy Rd. Alf DE55 .... B2
Croft Inf Sch. Alf DE55 ..... B2
Cross La. Shirl DE55 .... A4

Derby Rd. Alf DE55 .... A2
Derwent Gr. Alf DE55 .... A1
Dunsford Rd. Alf DE55 ..... B3

Each Well La. Alf DE55 .... A2
Ellesmere Ave. Alf DE55 .. B2
Elms Ave. Alf DE55 .... B2
Elms Cl. Alf DE55 .... B2
Elmwood Dr. Alf DE55 ...... C2
Ewart La. Alf DE55 .... A2

Firs Ave. Alf DE55 .... B3
Firs Gdns. Alf DE55 .... B2
Flowery Leys La. Alf ....
DE55 .... C2
Frederick St. Alf DE55 ...... B3

George St. Alf DE55 .... B2
Gladstone Rd. Alf DE55 ... A2
Gooker La. Alf DE55 .... A2
Grange St. Alf DE55 .... B2
Green The. Alf DE55 .... B2

Haddon Cl. Alf DE55 .... A2
Hall St. Alf DE55 .... B2
Hardy St. Alf DE55 .... A3
Henry Cres. Alf DE55 .... C2
High St. Alf DE55 .... B2
Hockley Way. Som DE55 .. B1

Independent Hill. Alf DE55 ..
.... A2
Institute La. Alf DE55 .... B2

John St. Alf DE55 .... B2

Keys Rd. Som DE55 .... B1
King St. Alf DE55 .... A2

Ley Ave. Alf DE55 .... B2
Ley Gdns. Alf DE55 .... B2
Leys Jun Sch. Alf DE55 .... C2
Limes Ave Alf DE55 .... B2
Lincoln St. Alf DE55 .... A2
Long Meadow Rd. Alf ....
DE55 .... A2
Lydford Rd. Alf DE55 .... B3

Mansfield Rd. Alf DE55 .... B2
Marshall St. Alf DE55 .... B2
Meadow Lane Alf DE55 ..... B3
Meadow Lane Ind Est. Alf
DE55 .... B3
Mercer Cres. Alf DE55 ..... C2
Milton Ave. Alf DE55 .... C2
Monk Rd. Som DE55 .... B1
Mortimer Wilson Sch. Alf
DE55 .... B2

New St. Alf DE55 .... B2
Normanton Ave. Alf DE55 C2
North St. Alf DE55 .... B2
Nottingham Rd. Alf DE55 . B1
Nuttall Cl. Alf DE55 .... A2
Nuttall St. Alf DE55 .... A2

Oak Dr. Alf DE55 .... B2
Oakland St. Alf DE55 .... B2
Orange St. Alf DE55 .... B2
Outseats Dr. Alf DE55 ...... B2

Park La. Shirl DE55 .... B4
Park Mill Dr. Black DE55 .. C4
Park St. Alf DE55 .... A2
Parkin St. Alf DE55 .... B2
Parkwood Sch. Alf DE55 .. A2
Pease Cl. Alf DE55 .... B2
Pease Hill. Alf DE55 .... B2
Pennytown Ct. Som DE55 C1
Prestom Ave. Alf DE55 ..... B2
Preston Ave. Alf DE55 ...... B2

Priory Rd. Alf DE55 .... B3
Prospect St. Alf DE55 .... B2
Providence Pl. Alf DE55 ... A2

Raglan St. Alf DE55 .... B2
Roberts Dr. Alf DE55 .... B2
Rodger's La. Alf DE55 ...... B3
Rowland Ct. Alf DE55 .... A2
Rowland St. Alf DE55 .... B2
Rugby Ave. Alf DE55 .... C2

Salcombe Rd. Alf DE55 .... C3
Severn Sq. Alf DE55 .... B2
Shakespeare Dr. Alf DE55 B2
Silver Birch Cres. Black ....
DE55 .... C4
Sleetmoor La. Alf DE55 .... A1
Smedley Ave. Som DE55 . C1
Southcroft. Alf DE55 .... B2

Tavistock Sq. Alf DE55 ..... B3
Trent Gr. Alf DE55 .... B1
Tribshelf Rd. Alf DE55 ...... C4

Venture Cres. Som DE55 . B1
Victoria St. Alf DE55 .... B2

Warwick Rd. Som DE55 ... C1
Watchorn La. Alf DE55 ..... A1
West End. Alf DE55 .... B2
West End Cl. Alf DE55 ...... B2
West Way. Som DE55 ...... C1
Wheatley Ave. Som DE55 ....
.... C1
Whites Cl. Som DE55 .... B1
Willow Cl. Alf DE55 .... B3
Willows Ave. Alf DE55 ..... B3
Wilson St. Alf DE55 .... B2
Wimsey Way. Som DE55 . B1
Wingfield Rd. Alf DE55 ..... A2
Wood St. Alf DE55 .... C3
Wood St N. Alf DE55 .... C3
Woodbridge Jun Sch. Alf
DE55 .... B2
Wycliffe Rd. Alf DE55 .... B2

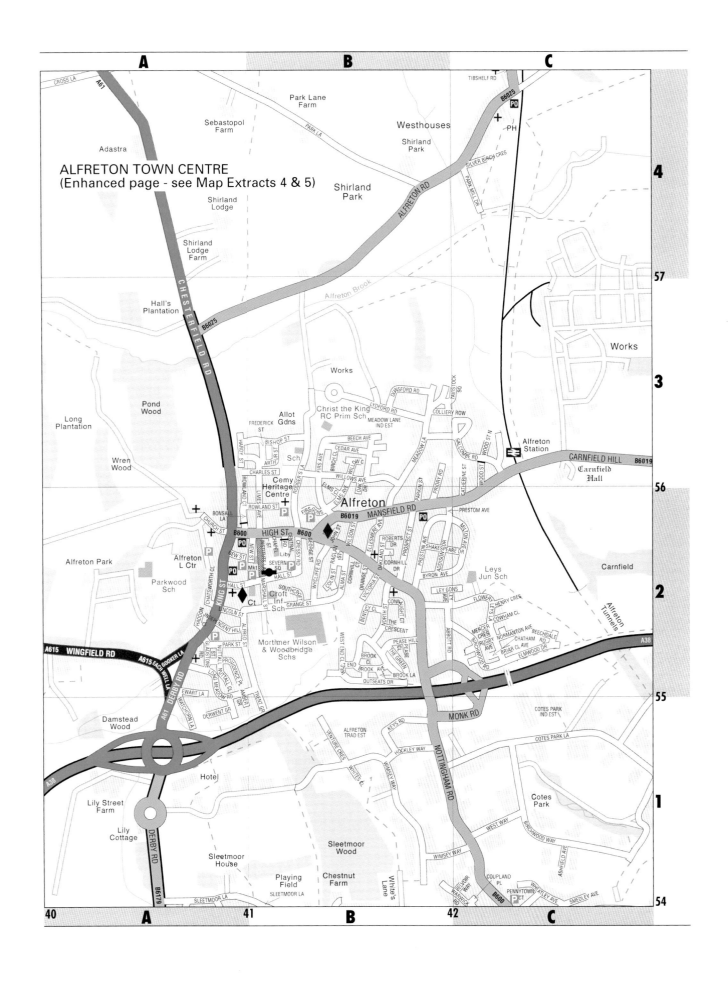

ALFRETON TOWN CENTRE
(Enhanced page - see Map Extracts 4 & 5)

Belper Gazetteer

Abbots Gr. Belper DE56 ...... B3
Acorn Dr. Belper DE56 .... B3
Acorn Way. Belper DE56 .... B3
Albert St. Belper DE56 .... A2
Alder Rd. Belper DE56 .... B2
Allstone Lee. Belper DE56 .. A3
Alport Cl. Belper DE56 .... B3
Alton Rd. Belper DE56 .... C2
Amber Ct. Belper DE56 .... B3
Appleton Dr. Belper DE56 ... B3
Applewood Cl. Belper DE56 B3
Arkwright Ave. Belper DE56 C3
Ash Acre. Belper DE56 .... C2
Ashford Rise. Belper DE56 .. C3
Ashton Way. Belper DE56 ... C2
Astlow Dr. Belper DE56 ...... B3
Avenue The. Belper DE56 ... A1

Babington Hospl. Belper ....
DE56 .... A1
Back Wyver La. Belper ....
DE56 .... A3
Bargate Cl. Belper DE56 ..... C1
Bargate Rd. Belper DE56 .. B1
Barley Croft. Belper DE56 .. B1
Barton Knoll. Belper DE56 .C2
Barton Knowle. Belper ....
DE56 .... C2
Beaurepaire Cres. Belper ....
DE56 .... B3
Becksitch La. Belper DE56 . A1
Beech Cl. Belper DE56 .... B2
Beechwood Cl. Belper DE56 ...
.... A3
Beeley Cl. Belper DE56 ...... C3
Belgrave Cl. Belper DE56 ... C3
Belle Acre Cl. Belper DE56 A2
Belper Rd Belper DE56 .... A1
Belper Sch. Belper DE56 .... C2
Belper Sports Ctr. Belper ....
DE56 .... C2
Belper Sta. Belper DE56 ..... A2
Bessalone Dr. Belper DE56 B3
Birchview Cl. Belper DE56 . B1
Blackbird Row. Holbr DE56 C1
Blenheim Ct. Belper DE56 .. A3
Bosley Mews. Belper DE56 A3
Bradley Dr. Belper DE56 .... B2
Bradshaw Croft. Belper DE56 .
.... A3
Bradwell Way. Belper DE56 B3
Brampton Ct. Belper DE56 .. C2
Bridge Foot. Belper DE56 ... A3
Bridge Hill. Belper DE56 .... A3
Bridge St. Belper DE56 .... A2
Broadholme La. Belper ....
DE56 .... B4
Brookside. Belper DE56 ..... A2
Broom Cl. Belper DE56 .... A3
Bullsmoor. Belper DE56 ..... C2
Burbage Cl. Belper DE56 .... C3
Bush Vale. Belper DE56 ..... A3
Butts The. Belper DE56 ...... B2

Calver Cl. Belper DE56 .... B3
Campbell St. Belper DE56 .. A2
Canada St. Belper DE56 ..... B1
Cedar Gr. Belper DE56 .... B1
Cemetery Rd. Belper DE56 . B3
Chapel St. Belper DE56 ..... A2
Charnwood Ave. Belper DE56
.... B2
Chatham Ct. Belper DE56 ... C2
Cheapside. Belper DE56 .... A2
Cherry Tree Ave. Belper ....
DE56 .... B3
Chesterfield Rd. Belper ....
DE56 .... B2
Chestnut Ave. Belper DE56 B1
Chevin Rd. Belper DE56 ..... A1
Chevin View. Belper DE56 .. A2
Church La. Belper DE56 ..... B2
Church St. Belper DE56 ...... B2
Cluster Rd. Belper DE56 ..... A2

Clusters The. Belper DE56 . A2
Coronation Ave. Belper DE56 .
.... B3
Courtney Way. Belper DE56 C3
Crich La. Belper DE56 .... B4
Croft The. Belper DE56 .... C1
Crown Terr. Belper DE56 .... A2
Culworth Cl. Belper DE56 ... C2

Days La. Belper DE56 .... A2
Deepdale Rd. Belper DE56 .. B3
Derby Rd Belper DE56 .... A1
Derwent Ave. Belper DE56 . B1
Derwent St. Belper DE56 .... A2
Derwent Vale. Belper DE56 A1
Derwent Valley Visitor Ctr.
Belper DE56 .... A3
Derwent View. Belper DE56 ..
.... A3
Dovedale Cres. Belper DE56 ..
.... B3
Dovedale Ct. Belper DE56 .. B2
Duncan Cl. Belper DE56 ..... B3

Edale Way. Belper DE56 ..... B3
Edensor Dr. Belper DE56 .... C3
Edward St. Belper DE56 ..... B2
Elm Ave. Belper DE56 .... B1
Elsecar Cl. Belper DE56 ..... C3
Eyam Wlk. Belper DE56 ..... B3

Falcons Rise. Belper DE56 . C3
Far Laund. Belper DE56 ...... B3
Farm Cl. Belper DE56 .... C2
Fellside. Belper DE56 .... B2
Field La. Belper DE56 .... A2
Field Row. Belper DE56 ..... A2
Findern Cl. Belper DE56 ..... C3
Fleet Cres. Belper DE56 ..... A2
Fleet Pk. Belper DE56 .... B2
Fleet The. Belper DE56 ...... A2
Ford St. Belper DE56 .... A2
Forest Cl. Belper DE56 ...... B3

George St. Belper DE56 ..... A2
Gibfield La. Belper DE56 ..... A1
Glen View. Belper DE56 ..... A1
Goods Rd. Belper DE56 ...... A1
Goods Yd. Belper DE56 ...... A1
Gorsey Cl. Belper DE56 ...... A3
Green La. Belper DE56 .... A2
Green The. Belper DE56 ..... B3
Gregorys Way. Belper DE56 C3

Harrier Rd. Belper DE56 ..... C3
Hawthorns The. Belper DE56 .
.... C3
Hayfield Cl. Belper DE56 .... B3
Herbert Strutt Prim Sch. ....
Belper DE56 .... A1
Heydon Cl. Belper DE56 ..... B3
High Edge Mews. Belper ....
DE56 .... B3
High Pavement. Belper ....
DE56 .... B2
High St. Belper DE56 .... B2
Highfield Rd. Belper DE56 . A1
Highwood Ave. Belper DE56 C1
Hillside Rise. Belper DE56 . A1
Holbrook Rd. Belper DE56 . A1
Honeycroft Cl. Belper DE56 B1
Hunter Rd. Belper DE56 ..... C3

Ingle's Channel. Belper DE56
.... A2

Jackson's La. Heage DE56 . C4
Jenny's Ct. Belper DE56 ..... C3
Jodrell Ave. Belper DE56 ... C2
John O'Gaunts Way. Belper ....
DE56 .... C2
Joseph St. Belper DE56 ...... A2
Jubilee Ct. Belper DE56 ..... B1

Kilburn Rd. Belper DE56 .... C2
King St. Belper DE56 .... A2
Kingswood Ave. Belper ....
DE56 .... C3
Kirk's La. Belper DE56 .... B2
Knowl Ave. Belper DE56 ..... A3

Ladywell Ct. Belper DE56 ... B2
Ladywood Ave. Belper DE56 ..
.... B3
Lander La. Belper DE56 ..... B2
Laund Ave. Belper DE56 ..... B3
Laund Cl. Belper DE56 .... B3
Laund Hill. Belper DE56 ..... B3
Laund Nook. Belper DE56 .. B3
Leche Cft. Belper DE56 ...... C2
Leonard Cheshire Cl Belper ....
DE56 .... B3
Leycote Way. Belper DE56 . B3
Leys Ct. Belper DE56 .... C2
Lime Cres. Belper DE56 ..... B1
Litton Cl. Belper DE56 .... B3
Lodge Dr. Belper DE56 ...... A3
Long Row. Belper DE56 ..... A2
Long Row Prim Sch. Belper ....
DE56 .... A3
Longstone Rise. Belper ....
DE56 .... B3
Lowlands Rd. Belper DE56 . B2

Maidwell Cl. Belper DE56 .. C3
Manor Rd. Belper DE56 ...... A2
Maple Dr. Belper DE56 ...... B1
Market Pl. Belper DE56 ...... B2
Marlborough Dr. Belper ....
DE56 .... C3
Marsh La. Belper DE56 ...... B3
Marsh Lane Cres. Belper ....
DE56 .... B2
Marston Cl. Belper DE56 .... C3
Martindale Ct. Belper DE56 C3
Matlock Rd. Belper DE56 ... A4
Meadow Ct. Belper DE56 ... A2
Meadow View Belper DE56 . A2
Melbourne Cl. Belper DE56 B1
Merlin Cl. Belper DE56 .... C3
Mill La. Belper DE56 .... B2
Mill St. Belper DE56 .... B2
Milldale Ct. Belper DE56 .... B2
Millers Dale Cl. Belper DE56 .
.... C3
Monyash Way. Belper DE56 ...
.... B3
Moulton Cl. Belper DE56 .... C3
Mount Pleasant Dr. Belper ......
DE56 .... A3
Mulberry Cl. Belper DE56 ... B2

Nailers Way. Belper DE56 .. C3
Naseby Rd. Belper DE56 ... C2
New Breck Rd. Belper DE56 ...
.... B2
New Rd. Belper DE56 .... A2
New Rd. Heage DE56 .... C4
Newton Cl. Belper DE56 ..... C3
Norbury Way. Belper DE56 . C3
Nottingham Rd. Belper DE56 .
.... B2

Openwoodgate. Belper DE56 .
.... C2
Orchard The. Belper DE56 .. B2
Orton Way. Belper DE56 ..... B3

Park Rd. Belper DE56 .... B1
Penn St. Belper DE56 .... B2
Pilsley Cl. Belper DE56 ...... C3
Pinchom's Hill Rd. Belper ......
DE56 .... B2
Pinewood Rd. Belper DE56 A3
Pinfold The. Belper DE56 ... C3
Pingle Cres. Belper DE56 ... A3
Pingle La. Belper DE56 ...... A3
Pottery Cl. Belper DE56 ...... C3

Pottery Prim Sch. Belper DE56
.... C2
Primary Cl. Belper DE56 .... B2
Prospect Dr. Belper DE56 ... A1
Pytchley Cl. Belper DE56 ... C2

Quarry Rd. Belper DE56 ..... A1
Queen St. Belper DE56 .... B2
Queen's Dr. Belper DE56 ... A3

Raven Oak Cl. Belper DE56 B2
River Gdns. Belper DE56 ... A3
Rothwell La. Belper DE56 .. B2
Royal Gate. Belper DE56 ... C2
Ryegrass Cl. Belper DE56 .. C2

St Elizabeth's RC Prim Sch. ...
Belper DE56 .... A3
St George's Pl. Belper DE56 ...
.... A2
St James Cl. Belper DE56 .. C2
St John's CE Prim Sch. Belper
DE56 .... B3
St John's Rd. Belper DE56 . B2
St Peter's Cl. Belper DE56 . A2
St Peters Croft. Belper DE56 ..
.... B2
Sandbed La. Belper DE56 .. C2
Scothches The. Belper DE56 ...
.... A3
Sherbourne Dr. Belper DE56 ..
.... C3
Short Lands. Belper DE56 .. B2
Short Row. Belper DE56 ..... A2
Short St. Belper DE56 .... B2
Snowberry Ave. Belper DE56 .
.... B2
Spencer Ave. Belper DE56 . B2
Spencer Rd. Belper DE56 .. B2
Spinners Way. Belper DE56 C3
Spinney The. Belper DE56 . B3
Spring Cl. Belper DE56 .... A3
Stanton Ave. Belper DE56 . B2
Strutt St. Belper DE56 .... A2
Sunny Bank Gdns. Belper ....
DE56 .... A1
Swinney Bank. Belper DE56 B3
Swinney La. Belper DE56 ... B3

Thorpe Way. Belper DE56 .. B3
Three Gates. Belper DE56 . A1

Valley View. Belper DE56 ... B1
Vicarage Cl. Belper DE56 ... B2

Walcote Cl. Belper DE56 .... C3
Walgrave Cl. Belper DE56 .. B3
Walnut Rd. Belper DE56 ..... B2
Warwick Gdns. Belper DE56 ...
.... C3
Weavers Cl. Belper DE56 ... C3
Wellington Ct. Belper DE56 A2
Welton Ave. Belper DE56 ... B3
Westbury Gdns. Belper DE56 ..
.... C3
Wheeldon Ave. Belper DE56 ...
.... B2
Whilton Ct. Belper DE56 ..... C2
Whitehouse Rise. Belper ....
DE56 .... A3
Whitemoor Hall. Belper DE56
.... C3
Whitemoor La. Belper DE56 ...
.... C3
Wicksteed Cl. Belper DE56 C3
Wilders Lea Ct. Belper ....
DE56 .... B1
William St. Belper DE56 ..... A2
Willow Gr. Belper DE56 ...... B1
Wilmot Rd. Belper DE56 ..... B2
Windmill La. Belper DE56 .. B2
Windmill Rise. Belper DE56 B3
Winster Cl. Belper DE56 ..... B3
Wyver La. Belper DE56 .... A4

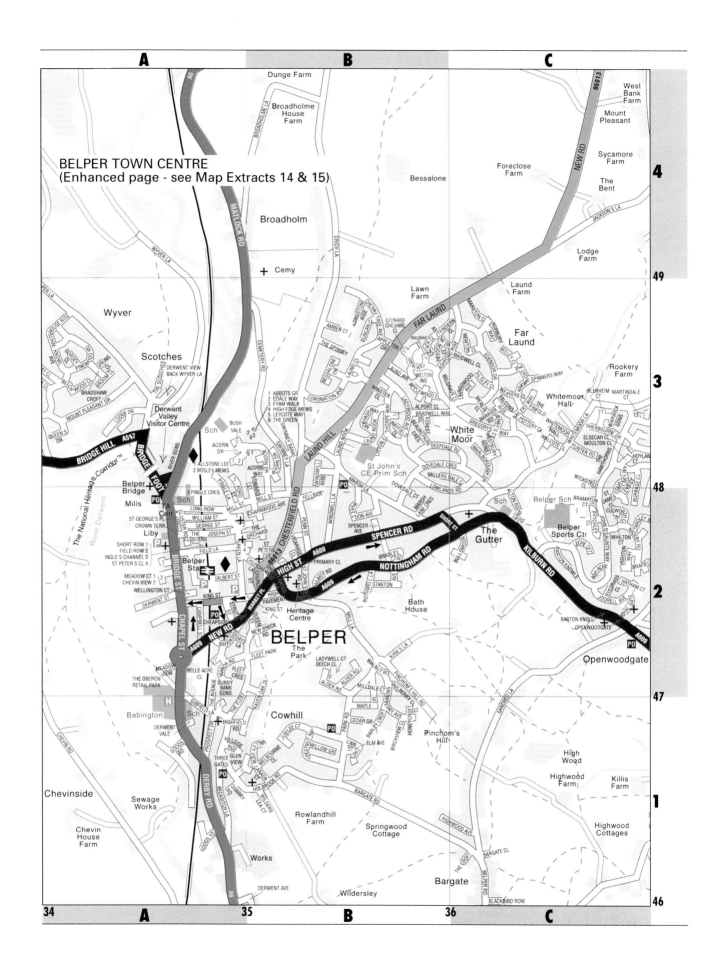

BELPER TOWN CENTRE
(Enhanced page - see Map Extracts 14 & 15)

Heanor Gazetteer

Abbott St. Hean DE75 .... B2
Adams Cl. Ship DE75 .... A1
Admiral Cl. Hean DE75 .... A2
Aldercar Inf Sch. Ald NG16 . C3
Aldercar La. Ald NG16 .... C4
Aldercar Sch. Ald NG16 ...... C3
Aldred's La. Hean DE75, ...
NG16 .... C2
Allandale Rd. Hean DE75.... A2
Amber Ct. Hean DE75 .... B2
Amber Dr. Hean NG16 .... C2
Andrews Dr. La Mill NG16 ... C3
Ardsley Cl. Hean DE75 .... C2
Ash Mount Rd. La Mill NG16 C3
Ashforth Ave. Hean DE75 ... C2
Astcote Cl. Hean DE75 .... C2
Avis Ave. Hean DE75 .... B1

Bailey Brook Cres. La Mill ....
NG16 .... C3
Bailey Brook Dr. La Mill ....
NG16 .... C3
Bailey Brook Ind Est. Hean .....
DE75 .... C2
Bailey Brook Wlk. La Mill ....
NG16 .... C3
Baker Ave. Hean DE75 .... B1
Balmoral Cl. Hean DE75 ...... A2
Banksburn Cl. Hean DE75 ... B2
Bassford Ave. Hean DE75 ... B2
Beeches The. Hean DE75 .... A1
Belfield Ct. Hean DE75 .... A3
Berle Ave. Hean DE75 .... B2
Bestwick Ave. Hean DE75 ... C2
Birchfield Pk. Hean DE75 .... B1
Birchwood. Hean DE75 .... A3
Bircumshaw's Rd. Hean ....
DE75 .... B2
Brampton Ave. Hean DE75 .. C2
Breach Rd. Hean DE75 .... C1
Broadway. Hean DE75 .... B2
Brockhall Rise. Hean DE75 . C2
Brook Ct. Hean NG16 .... C2
Brookfield Way. Hean DE75 C2
Brooklands Ave. Hean DE75 ...
.... B2
Burns St. Hean DE75 .... A2
Burnt House Rd. Hean DE75 ...
.... A2
Burton St. Hean DE75.......... B2
Buxton Ave. Hean DE75....... B1

Calladine Rd. Hean DE75.... A2
Carlton Cl. Hean DE75 .... C3
Carlyle Pl. Hean DE75 .... A3
Carlyle St. Hean DE75 .... A3
Carrock Ave. Hean DE75 .... C2
Castle View. Ald NG16 .... C3
Chapel St. Hean DE75 .... C1
Chestnut Bank. Hean DE75 . A2
Chestnut Rd. La Mill NG16 .. C3
Church Sq. Hean DE75 .... B2
Church St. Hean DE75 .... B2
Clara Mount Rd. Hean DE75 C2
Clarke Ave. Hean DE75 .... A2
Claxton St. Hean DE75 .... A2
Claxton Terr. Hean DE75 ..... A2
Clay La. Hean DE75 .... B2
Clayton Gr. Hean DE75 .... A3
Coppice Dr. Hean DE75 .... B1
Coppice Prim Sch. Hean ....
DE75 .... B1
Corfield Ave. Hean DE75 ..... B1
Cornfield CE Inf Sch. Hean ......
DE75 .... A2
Cottage Garden La. Hean ....
DE75 .... A2
Cromford Cl. Ald NG16........ C3
Darfield Dr. Hean DE75 .... B4
Cromford Rd. La Mill NG16 . C3

Daltons Cl. Ald NG16 .... C3
Darfield Dr. Hean DE75 .... C2
Deepdale Ct. Hean DE75 ..... B2
Delves Rd. Hean DE75 .... A1
Derby Rd. Hean DE75 .... A2

Derby Road Ind Est. Hean ....
DE75 .... A2
Dodford Ct. Hean DE75 .... C2
Douglas Ave. Hean DE75 .... A2
Draycott Cl. Hean DE75 .... A3

East Nelson St. Hean DE75 . B2
East St. Hean DE75 .... C1
Ebenezer St. La Mill NG16 .. C3
Edward St. Ald NG16 .... C3
Egreaves Ave. Hean DE75 .. A3
Ella Bank Rd. Hean DE75 .... C2
Elmsfield Ave. Hean DE75 .. C2
England Cres. Hean DE75 ... C2

Fall Rd. Hean DE75 .... B3
Flamstead Ave. Hean DE75.. A3
Fletcher St. Hean DE75 .... B2
Ford Ave. Hean DE75 .... A3
Frederic Ave. Hean DE75 .... B1
Frost Ave. La Mill NG16 ...... C3
Furnace La. Hean DE75 ...... A3

Gardens The. Hean DE75 .... A3
Garnett Ave. Hean DE75 ...... B2
George St. La Mill NG16 ..... C3
Gillot St. Hean DE75 .... C1
Gladstone Ave. Hean DE75 . B2
Gladstone St. Hean DE75 ... B2
Godfrey St. Hean DE75 .... B2
Godkin Dr. Ald NG16 .... C3
Grace Cres. Hean DE75 ...... B2
Grandfield St. Hean DE75 ... A3
Grange The. Smal DE75 ...... A1
Greenacre Ave. Hean DE75 . C3
Greenfields. Ald NG16 .... C3
Gregg Ave. Hean DE75 .... B2
Gregory Ave. Ald NG16 .... C3
Gregory Ave. La Mill NG16 .. C3
Groome Ave. Hean DE75 ..... A3

Hallington Dr. Hean DE75 ... A2
Hamlet The. Hean DE75 ...... B3
Hand's Rd. Hean DE75 .... C2
Hardy Barn. Ship DE75 .... C1
Harold Ave. Ald NG16 .... C3
Hassock La N. Ship DE75 ... C1
Hazel Cl. Hean DE75 .... A2
Heanor Gate Ind Est. Hean .....
DE75 .... A1
Heanor Gate Rd. Hean DE75 A1
Heanor Gate Sch. Hean ....
DE75 .... A2
Heanor Langley Mill & District
Meml Hospl. Hean DE75 ..... B2
Heanor Rd. Hean DE75 .... A2
Heanor Rd. Hean DE75 .... A3
Heyford Ct. Hean DE75 .... C2
High St. Hean DE75 .... A3
High St. Hean DE75 .... B2
Highgrove Cl. Hean DE75.... A2
Hill Rd. Hean DE75 .... A2
Hillside. La Mill NG16 .... C3
Hoggbarn La. Hean NG16 ... A4
Holbrook St. Hean DE75 ..... C2
Holmes Cl. La Mill NG16 .... C3
Holmes St. Hean DE75 .... A2
Holmesfield Dr. Ship DE75 . C1
Homestead. Ald NG16 .... C3
Horsley Cres. La Mill NG16 . C3
Howitt St. Hean DE75 .... B2
Hufton's Ct. Ship DE75 .... C1
Hufton's Dr. Ship DE75 .... C1
Hunt Ave. Hean DE75 .... B2

Ilkeston Rd. Hean DE75 ...... B1

Joan Ave. Hean DE75 .... B2
John St. Hean DE75 .... A2
Johnson Dr. Hean DE75 ...... B2
Julie Ave. Hean DE75 .... C2

Kensington Ave. Hean DE75 A2
Kew Cres. Hean DE75 .... C2
Kings Cl. Hean DE75 .... A2
Kingsway. Hean DE75 .... A2

Kirkham Cl. Hean DE75 .... A2
Kirkman Rd. Hean DE75 ...... A3
Lacey Fields Rd. Hean ....
DE75 .... C2
Lake Ave. Hean DE75 .... A3
Langley Inf Sch. Hean DE75 C2
Langley Mill CE Inf Sch. ....
La Mill NG16 .... C3
Langley Mill Jun Sch. Ald ....
NG16 .... C3
Langley Mill Sta. Hean ....
NG16 .... C3
Langley Pk. La Mill NG16 .... C3
Lawn Cl. Hean DE75 .... B2
Leafy La. Hean DE75 .... B2
Lee La. Hean DE75 .... C2
Leniscar Ave. Hean DE75 .... A3
Leonard Cheshire Cl. Hean .....
DE75 .... C2
Lilac Gr. Hean DE75 .... B2
Lockton Ave. Hean DE75 ..... B1
Longbridge La. Hean DE75 . A3
Loscoe Grange. Hean DE75 A3
Loscoe Rd. Hean DE75 .... A2
Lower Clara Mount Rd. Hean ...
DE75 .... C2
Lower Dunstead Rd. Ald ....
NG16 .... C3
Lower Dunstead Rd. La Mill ....
NG16 .... C3
Lower Gladstone St. Hean ......
DE75 .... B2
Lower Maples. Hean DE75 .. C1
Lower Nelson St. Hean ....
DE75 .... A2
Lowlands Lea. Hean DE75 .. B2

Mansfield Rd. Hean DE75 ... C2
Maple Gdns. Hean DE75 ..... A2
Market St. Hean DE75 .... B2
Marlpool Inf Sch. Hean ....
DE75 .... C1
Marlpool Jun Sch. Hean ....
DE75 .... C2
Marshall St. Hean DE75 ...... B2
Mary Howitt Inf Com Sch. ....
Hean DE75 .... A2
Mayfield Ave. Hean DE75 ... B2
Meadows The. Hean DE75 .. B2
Midland Rd. Hean DE75 ...... B2
Mill Rd. Hean DE75 .... C1
Millbank. Hean DE75 .... C1
Milward Rd. Hean DE75 ...... A2
Mitchell Ave. La Mill NG16 . C3
Mount St. Hean DE75 .... B2
Mundy CE Jun Sch. Hean ....
DE75 .... B2
Mundy St. Hean DE75 .... B2
Mundy's Dr. Hean DE75 ...... B1

Neal Ct. La Mill NG16 .... C3
Newham Cl. Hean DE75 ...... C2
Newlands Dr. Hean DE75 .... B3
Nook End Rd. Hean DE75 ... A2
Nook The. Hean DE75 .... A3
North St. La Mill NG16 .... C3
Northern Rd. Hean DE75 ..... A2

Oak Ave. Ald NG16 .... C4
Oaklands Ave. Hean DE75 .. C2
Old Coppice Side. Hean ....
DE75 .... B1
Old Pond The. Hean DE75 .. C1
Oliver Cl. Hean DE75 .... C2
Orchard Ct. La Mill NG16 ... C3
Orchard Rise. Hean DE75 ... B2
Orchard St. La Mill NG16 .... C3
Ormonde St. Ald NG16 .... C3
Ormonde Terr. Ald NG16 .... C3
Owers Ave. Hean DE75 .... B1

Park Ct. Hean DE75 .... B2
Park St. Hean DE75 .... A2
Park View. Hean DE75 .... A2
Peach St. Hean DE75 .... A2
Peatburn Ave. Hean DE75 ... A2

Peel St. La Mill NG16 .... C3
Pine Ave. La Mill NG16 .... C3
Platts Ave. Hean DE75 .... A2
Plumptre. Ald NG16 .... C4
Poynter Cl. Hean DE75 .... A2
Prospect Rd. Hean DE75 .... C1
Purchase Ave. Hean DE75 ... A2

Queens Ave. Hean DE75 ..... A2

Ray St. Hean DE75 .... B2
Ray's Ave. Hean DE75 .... B2
Red Lion Sq. Hean DE75 ..... B2
Regent St. La Mill NG16 ...... C3
Ridgeway. Hean DE75 .... B1
Roper Ave. Hean DE75 .... B1
Ropewalk The. Hean DE75 .. B1
Rosewood Cres. Hean DE75 C2

St Lawrence Cl. Hean DE75 B2
Sawmills Ind Pk. Hean ....
DE75 .... A3
Saxton Ave. Hean DE75 ...... B2
Sedgwick St. La Mill NG16 .. C3
Sheldon Rd. Hean DE75 ...... A4
Shipley Ctry Pk Visitor Ctr. .....
Ship DE75 .... B1
Sinclair Cl. Hean DE75 .... A1
Slack La. Ship DE75 .... B1
Smeeton St. Hean DE75 ..... C2
Smith Dr. La Mill NG16 .... C3
South East Derbyshire Coll. ....
Hean DE75 .... B2
Sovereign Way. Hean DE75 A2
Spring La. Hean DE75 .... B2
Stainsby Ave. Hean DE75 ... B1
Stamford St. Hean DE75 ..... B2
Starthe Bank. Hean DE75 ... B2
Station Rd. Hean NG16 .... C2
Station Rd. La Mill NG16 ..... C2
Stoddard Dr. Hean DE75 ..... B2
Sunningdale Ave. Hean ....
DE75 .... B1

Tantum Ave. Hean DE75 ..... A3
Taylor La. Hean DE75 .... A3
Thistle Green Cl. Hean DE75 C2
Thompson St. La Mill NG16 C3
Thorpe Hill Dr. Hean DE75 .. B1
Thorpe's Rd. Hean DE75 ..... A2
Thorpe's Rd. Ship DE75 ...... A1
Tudor Falls. Hean DE75 ...... B3
Turner Ave. La Mill NG16 .... C3
Turton Cl. La Mill NG16 .... C3
Twyford Cl. Hean DE75 .... A1

Upper Barn Cl. Hean DE75 .. B2
Upper Dunstead Rd. Ald ....
NG16 .... C3
Upper Nelson St. Hean DE75 A2
Upton Cl. Hean DE75 .... C2

Vicarage Gdns. Hean DE75 . B2
Victoria Ave. Hean DE75 ..... A2

Watkinson St. Hean DE75 ... A2
Watson Ave. Hean DE75 ..... B2
Wellington St. Hean DE75 ... A3
Wentworth Croft. Hean ....
DE75 .... C3
West St. Hean DE75 .... A2
West St. La Mill NG16 .... C3
Western Dr. Hean DE75 ...... B1
Westfield Ave. Hean DE75 .. B2
Weston St. Hean DE75 .... C1
Whysall St. Hean DE75 .... B2
William Howitt Jun Com Sch. ...
Hean DE75 .... A2
Wilmot St. Hean DE75 .... B2
Windsor Cl. Hean DE75 .... B3
Wood End Rd. Hean DE75 .. B2

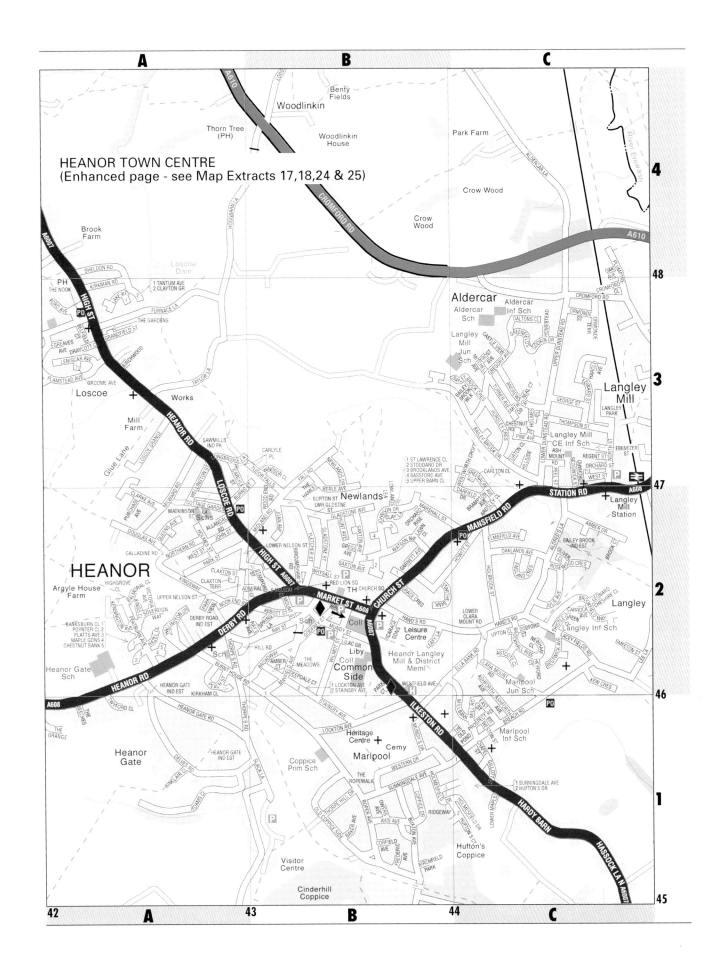

Ripley Gazetteer

Albert Rd. Ripley DE5 .... A3
Albert St. Ripley DE5 .... B3
Albion St. Ripley DE5 .... B3
Alfred St. Ripley DE5 .... B3
Allissa Ave. Ripley DE5 .... B2
Alma St. Ripley DE5 .... A4
Almond Ave. Ripley DE5 .. A2
Amber Hts. Ripley DE5 ..... A3
Argyll Rd. Ripley DE5 .... B3
Ash Cres. Ripley DE5 .... A2

Ballacraine Dr. Ripley ....
DE5 .... B3
Bamford St. Ripley DE5 .... A2
Beech Ave. Ripley DE5 ..... A3
Beighton St. Ripley DE5 ... B3
Belle Vue Ave. Ripley DE5 A1
Belton Dr. Ripley DE5 .... B3
Benjamin Outram Bsns Ctr. ...
Ripley DE5 .... B2
Bideford Cl. Ripley DE5 .... A3
Birch Cl. Ripley DE5 .... A2
Bolsover Cl. Ripley DE5 ... B3
Booth St. Ripley DE5 .... B3
Bowler St. Ripley DE5 ...... A2
Briars Way. Ripley DE5 .... A2
Brickyard La. Ripley DE5 . B3
Bridle La. Ripley DE5 .... B3
Britannia Ave. Ripley DE5 C2
Brittain Dr. Ripley DE5 ..... C3
Broadway. Ripley DE5 ...... B3
Broadway Ave. Ripley DE5 B3
Broadway Ct. Ripley DE5 . B3
Brook La. Ripley DE5 .... A2
Brook St. Hean DE75 .... C1
Brookfield Cl. Codnor ....
DE5 .... C3
Brookvale Ave. Codnor ....
DE5 .... C2
Butterley Croft Bsns Ctr. ....
Ripley DE5 .... B2
Butterley Hill. Ripley DE5 B4
Butterley La. Ripley DE5 .. A4

Calke Rise. Ripley DE5 .... B3
Cavendish Dr. Ripley DE5 A3
Cedar Ave. Ripley DE5 ..... A3
Cemetery La. Ripley DE5 . B3
Chapel St. Ripley DE5 ...... A1
Charnwood Dr. Ripley DE5 A3
Cherry Tree Ave. Ripley ....
DE5 .... A2
Chestnut Ave. Ripley DE5 . A2
Church Croft. Ripley DE5 .. A3
Church St. Ripley DE5 ...... A3
Church St. Ripley DE5 ...... C2
Coach Rd. Ripley DE5 ...... B4
Cobden St. Ripley DE5 ..... A3
Codnor CE Prim Sch. Codnor
DE5 .... C2
Codnor Denby La. Codnor .....
DE5 .... C11
Codnor Gate. Codnor DE5 C3
Codnor Gate Ind Est. Ripley ..
DE5 .... C3
Colin Ave. Codnor DE5 ..... C2
Cooper St. Ripley DE5 ...... A3
Coupe St. Ripley DE5 .... B2
Cromford Rd. Ripley DE5 . A3
Cross La. Codnor DE5 ...... C2
Crosshill. Codnor DE5 ...... C1
Crossley St. Ripley DE5 ... A3

Dannah Cres. Ripley DE5 . B3
Dannah St. Ripley DE5 ..... B3
Darley Dr. Ripley DE5 ...... A4
Derby Rd. Ripley DE5 .... A3
Derwent Rd. Ripley DE5 ... A3
Devonshire Ave. Ripley DE5 ..
.... A3
Dove Rd. Ripley DE5 .... A3

Dovedale Cl. Ripley DE5 .. A1

Eastfield Rd. Ripley DE5 .. C3
Elms Ave. Ripley DE5 .... A2
Emmas Williams Ct. Ripley
DE5 .... A3

Fearn Ave. Ripley DE5 ..... B3
Ferrers Way. Ripley DE5 .. A4
Field St. Codnor DE5 .... C2
Field Terr. Ripley DE5 ...... A3
Firs Ave. Ripley DE5 .... A3
Fletcher's Row. Ripley ....
DE5 .... B3
Fletcher St. Ripley DE5 .... B3
Ford Cl. Ripley DE5 .... A2
Foresters Way. Ripley ....
.... A3
Forty Horse Cl. Ripley ....
DE5 .... C3

Gardens The. Ripley DE5 . A2
Gate Brook Cl. Codnor ....
DE5 .... C3
Glasshouse Hill. Codnor ......
DE5 .... C2
Glebe Ave. Ripley DE5 ..... A3
Glen Vine. Ripley DE5 ...... C3
Greaves St. Ripley DE5 .... B3
Greenhill Ave. Ripley DE5 B2
Grenvoir Dr. Ripley DE5 ... C3
Grosvenor Rd. Ripley DE5 A3
Grove Ct. Ripley DE5 .... B2

Hammersmith. Ripley DE5 ....
.... A4
Hardwick Cl. Ripley DE5 .. A4
Hardy Cres. Codnor DE5 .. C2
Harris Ave. Ripley DE5 ..... A3
Harris Cl. Ripley DE5 .... A3
Hartshay Hill. Ripley DE5 . A3
Havelock St. Ripley DE5 ... B3
Hawthorn Ave. Ripley DE5 A2
Hazeltree Cl. Ripley DE5 .. A2
Heage Rd. Ripley DE5 ...... A3
Heanor Rd. Codnor DE5 ... C2
Heath Rd. Ripley DE5 .... B3
Henry St. Ripley DE5 .... A3
Hickleton Cl. Ripley DE5 .. A3
High Holborn Rd. Codnor......
DE5 .... C3
High Holborn Rd. Ripley ......
DE5 .... C3
High Meadow Cl. Ripley ....
DE5 .... A2
High St. Ripley DE5 .... A3
High St. Codnor DE5 .... C2
Highfield Cl. Hean DE75 ... C1
Highfield Way. Ripley DE5 A2
Highfields. Codnor DE5 .... C2
Hill St. Ripley DE5 .... A4
Hillberry. Ripley DE5 .... C3
Hillcrest Dr. Codnor DE5 .. C2
Holborn View. Codnor ....
DE5 .... C3
Holly Ave. Ripley DE5 ...... A2
Hollywell Ave. Codnor ....
DE5 .... C2
Honeyfield Dr. Ripley DE5 B2

Ivy Gr. Ripley DE5 .... A3

Jessop St. Codnor DE5 .... C2
Jessop St. Ripley DE5 ...... C2
Jubilee Ave. Ripley DE5 ... A3
Jura Ave. Ripley DE5 .... A3

Kedleston Cl. Ripley DE5 . A4
Kenilworth Rd. Ripley DE5 A3
Kepple Gate. Ripley DE5 .. B2
Kirk Cl. Ripley DE5 .... A2

Lamb Cres. Ripley DE5 .... B3
Larch Ave. Ripley DE5 ...... A3
Lathkill Dr. Ripley DE5 ..... A1
Laurel Ave. Ripley DE5 .... A3
Lawrence Ave. Ripley DE5 A2
Leamington St. Ripley ....
DE5 .... B3
Ledo Ave. Ripley DE5 .... A3
Lime Ave. Ripley DE5 .... A3
Limes Pk. Ripley DE5 .... A3
Long Cl. Ripley DE5 .... B2
Lons Inf Sch. Ripley DE5 .. A3
Lowes Hill. Ripley DE5 ..... A4
Lyncroft Ave. Ripley DE5 .. B3
Lyndale Dr. Codnor DE5 ... C2
Lynton Cl. Ripley DE5 .... A4

Manor Croft. Ripley DE5 ... A4
Manvers Ave. Ripley DE5 . B3
Manvers St. Ripley DE5 .... B3
Maple Ave. Ripley DE5 ..... A2
Market Pl. Ripley DE5 .... A3
Meadow Ave. Codnor DE5 C2
Meadow Rd. Ripley DE5 ... B3
Middleton Ave. Codnor ....
DE5 .... C1
Midland Railway Ctr. Ripley
DE5 .... B4
Mill Hil Sch. Ripley DE5 ... B2
Mill La. Codnor DE5 .... C2
Milldale Cl. Ripley DE5 ..... A1
Milner Ave. Codnor DE5 ... C2
Morleyfields Cl. Ripley ....
DE5 .... B3
Moseley St. Ripley DE5 .... A3
Moss La. Ripley DE5 .... A4
Mount Pleasant. Ripley ....
DE5 .... A3
Mulberry Mews. Ripley ....
DE5 .... A1

Needham St. Codnor DE5 C2
New St. Ripley DE5 .... B3
Newham Ave. Ripley DE5 . A3
Nightingale Cl. Ripley ....
DE5 .... A3
Norman Rd. Ripley DE5 ... A3
Northam Dr. Ripley DE5 ... A4
Nottingham Rd. Ripley ....
DE5 .... B3

Oak Ave. Ripley DE5 .... A2
Old Hartshay Hill. Ripley ......
DE5 .... A3
Orchard Cl. Ripley DE5 .... C2
Orchard The. Codnor DE5 C3
Outram Ct. Ripley DE5 ..... B3
Outram St. Ripley DE5 ..... B3
Oxford St. Ripley DE5 .... A3

Padley Cl. Ripley DE5 .... A4
Park Ave. Ripley DE5 .... B3
Park Rd. Ripley DE5 .... B3
Park St. Ripley DE5 .... B3
Pasteur Ave. Ripley DE5 .. A3
Peakdale Cl. Ripley DE5 .. A1
Pear Tree Ave. Ripley DE5 A2
Peasehill. Ripley DE5 .... B2
Peasehill Rd. Ripley DE5 . B2
Pentrich Rd. Ripley DE5 ... A3
Peveril Ct. Ripley DE5 ...... A3
Pine Cl. Ripley DE5 .... A3
Pinewood Ave. Codnor..........
DE5 .... C2
Pit Farm. Ripley DE55 ...... C4
Pit La. Ripley DE5 .... B3
Pit La. Codnor DE5 .... C2
Poplar Ave. Ripley DE5 .... A2
Porterhouse Rd. Ripley ....
DE5 .... B3
Providence St. Ripley DE5 B2

Queen St. Ripley DE5 .... C2
Queensview Dr. Ripley ....
DE5 .... C2
Quenby La. Ripley DE5 ..... B3

Redfern Ave. Ripley DE5 .. B3
Redmoor Cl. Codnor DE5 . C3
Reynolds Ave. Ripley DE5 B3
Ridgedale View. Ripley ....
DE5 .... A3
Ripley Hospl. Ripley DE5 . A3
Ripley Inf Sch. Ripley DE5 A2
Ripley Jun Sch. Ripley ....
DE5 .... A2
Rowan Ave. Ripley DE5 .... A2
Rutland Ave. Ripley DE5 .. C2

St John's CE Prim Sch. ....
Ripley DE5 .... B3
St Johns Cl. Ripley DE5 .... B3
Samuel Ct. Ripley DE5 ..... A2
Sandham La. Ripley DE5 . A3
School La. Ripley DE5 ...... A3
Shirley Rd. Ripley DE5 ..... A3
Slack La. Ripley DE5 .... A3
Smith Ave. Codnor DE5 .... C3
South Pl. Ripley DE5 .... A3
Spinney The. Ripley DE5 .. A4
Springfield Ave. Hean ....
DE75 .... C1
Springfield Terr. Ripley ....
DE5 .... B3
Springfield View. Ripley ....
DE5 .... A3
Springhill Way. Codnor ....
DE5 .... C2
Stanley Ave. Ripley DE5 ... B3
Station La. Codnor DE5 .... C1
Steam Mill La. Ripley DE5 C2
Stirland St. Codnor DE5 ... C3
Strelley Ave. Ripley DE5 .. A2
Sycamore Ave. Ripley DE5 A2

Tavistock Ave. Ripley DE5 A3
Thomson Dr. Codnor DE5 . C2
Thoresby Cl. Ripley DE5 ... B3

Upper Marehay Rd. ....
Ripley DE5 .... A1

Victoria Rd. Ripley DE5 .... A3
Victoria St. Ripley DE5 ..... B3
Victory Ave. Ripley DE5 ... B3

Waingroves Prim Sch. ....
Ripley DE5 .... C2
Waingroves Rd. Codnor ....
DE5 .... C1
Waingroves Rd. Ripley ....
DE5 .... C2
Walker Ave. Ripley DE5 ... B3
Wall St. Ripley DE5 .... A3
Warmwells La. Ripley ....
DE5 .... A1
Well St. Ripley DE5 .... A3
Wellington St. Ripley DE5 B3
West Ave. Ripley DE5 .... A3
West Hill. Codnor DE5 ...... C2
Weston Spot Cl. Ripley ....
DE5 .... A2
Whitcombe Pl. Ripley DE5 A3
White Gates. Codnor DE5 C2
Whiteley Rd. Ripley DE5 .. B2
Willow Ave. Ripley DE5 .... A2
Wood St. Ripley DE5 .... B3
Wood St. Codnor DE5 ...... C2
Woodfield Dr. Ripley DE5 . C2
Woodside Ave. Ripley ....
DE5 .... A2
Wright Ave. Ripley DE5 .... B3
Wright St. Codnor DE5 ..... C2

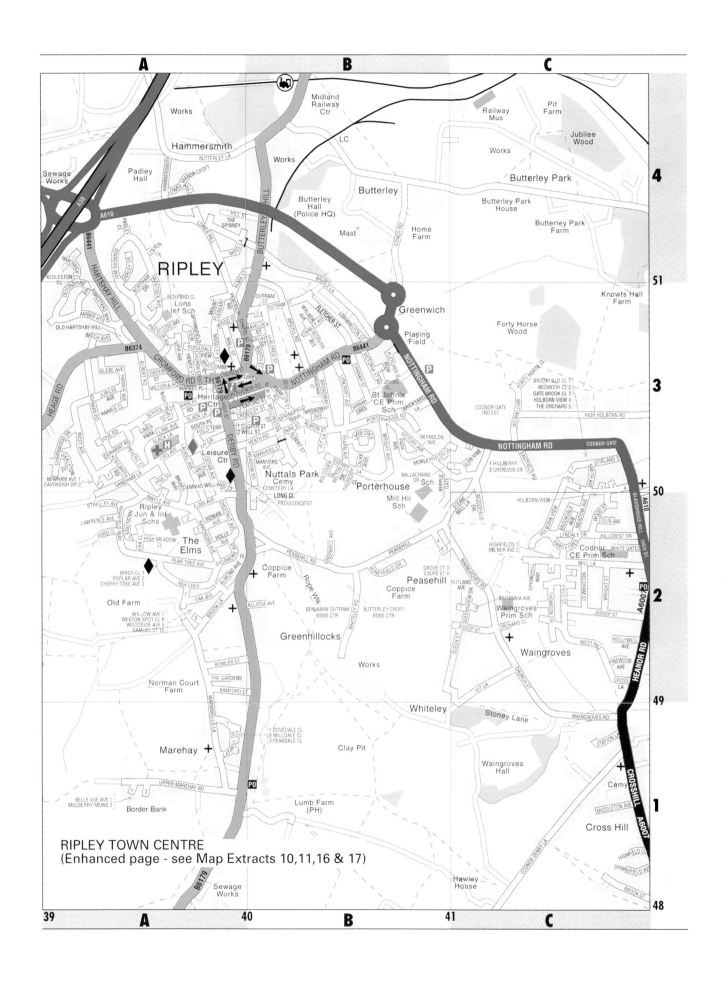

RIPLEY TOWN CENTRE
(Enhanced page - see Map Extracts 10,11,16 & 17)

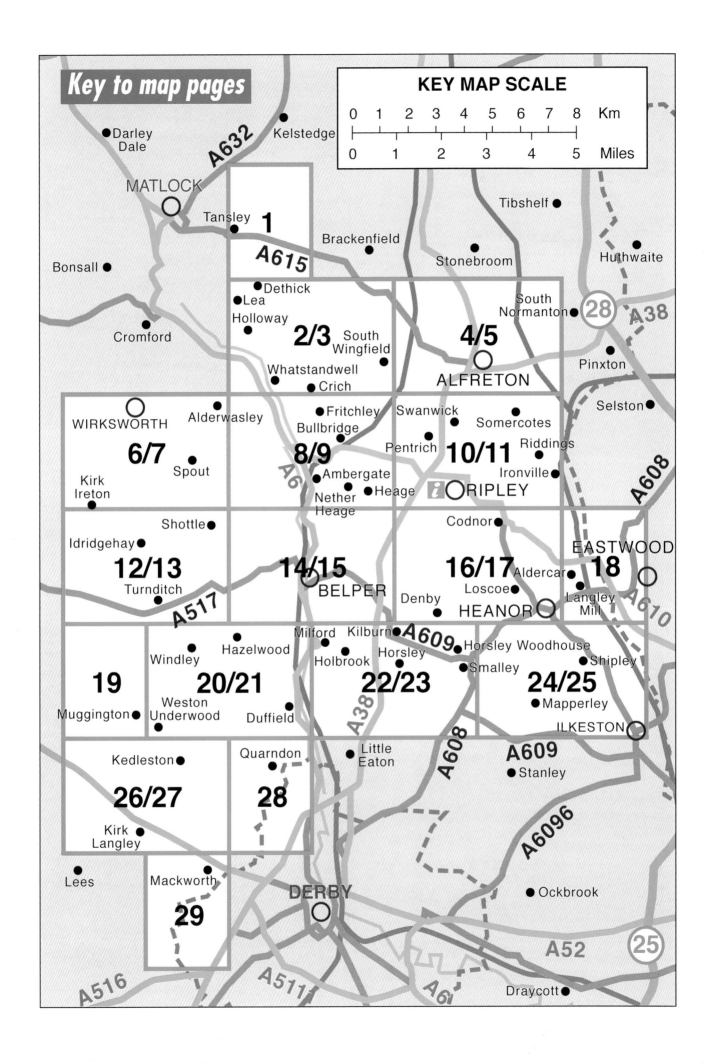

Key to map pages

KEY MAP SCALE

| 0 | 1 | 2 | 3 | 4 | 5 | 6 | 7 | 8 | Km |

| 0 | 1 | 2 | 3 | 4 | 5 | Miles |

Darley
Dale

Kelstedge

A632

MATLOCK

Tansley

1

Brackenfield

Tibshelf

A615

Bonsall

Stonebroom

Huthwaite

Dethick

Lea

Holloway

2/3 South
Wingfield

South
Normanton

4/5

28

A38

Cromford

Whatstandwell

ALFRETON

Pinxton

Crich

Selston

Fritchley

Swanwick

WIRKSWORTH

Alderwasley

Bullbridge

Somercotes

6/7

Spout

Pentrich

8/9

10/11

Riddings

Kirk
Ireton

Ambergate

Ironville

A6

Heage

i RIPLEY

A608

Nether
Heage

Shottle

Codnor

Idridgehay

EASTWOOD

12/13

14/15

16/17 Aldercar

18

Turnditch

BELPER

Loscoe

Langley
Mill

A517

Denby

HEANOR

A610

Milford

Kilburn

A609

Horsley Woodhouse

Hazelwood

Holbrook

Horsley

Smalley

Shipley

Windley

19

20/21

22/23

24/25

Weston
Underwood

A38

Mapperley

Muggington

Duffield

A608

ILKESTON

Kedleston

Quarndon

Little
Eaton

A609

Stanley

26/27

28

A6096

Kirk
Langley

Lees

Mackworth

Ockbrook

DERBY

29

A52

25

A516

A5111

A6

Draycott

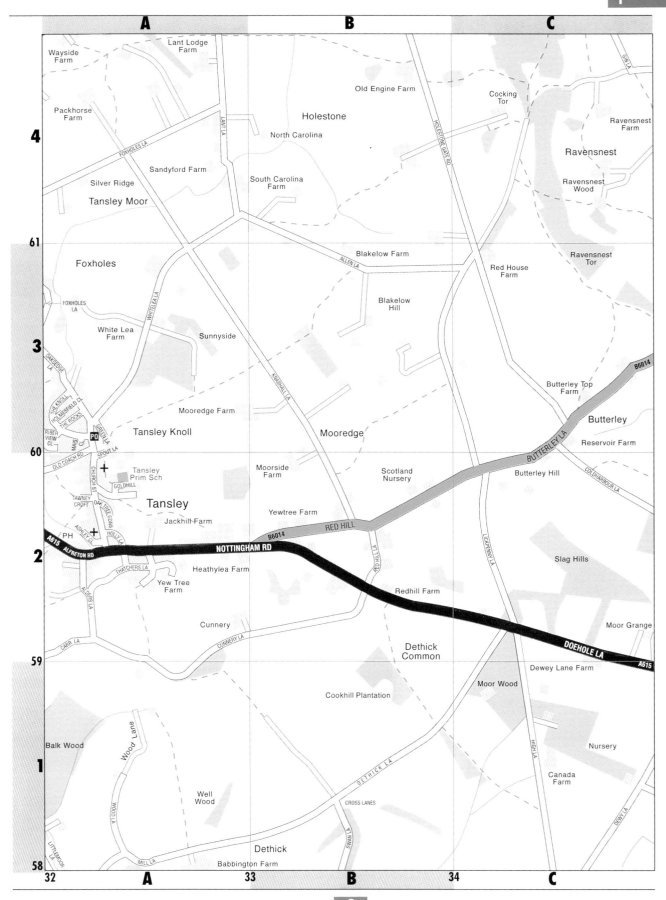

A   B   C

Wayside
Farm

Lant Lodge
Farm

Old Engine Farm

Cocking
Tor

Ravensnest
Farm

Packhorse
Farm

Holestone

4

North Carolina

Ravensnest

Sandyford Farm

Ravensnest
Wood

Silver Ridge

South Carolina
Farm

Tansley Moor

61

Foxholes

Blakelow Farm

Red House
Farm

Ravensnest
Tor

FOXHOLES
LA

Blakelow
Hill

White Lea
Farm

Butterley Top
Farm

B6014

Sunnyside

3

OAKSEDGE LA

Mooredge Farm

Butterley

THE KNOLL

HOLMESFIELD CL

THE ROCKS

Tansley Knoll

Mooredge

Reservoir Farm

RIBER
VIEW
CL

PO

GREEN LA

60

Butterley Hill

COLDHARBOUR LA

Old Coach Rd

SPOUT LA

Tansley
Prim Sch

Moorside
Farm

Scotland
Nursery

GOLDHILL

TAWNEY
CROFT

Tansley

Jackhill Farm

Yewtree Farm

Slag Hills

CHURCH ST

OAK TREE GDNS

2

PH

A615 ALFRETON RD

NOTTINGHAM RD

B6014   RED HILL

RED HILL LA

LICKPENNY LA

Moor Grange

HOLLY LA

ASHLEY CL

THATCHERS LA

Heathylea Farm

Redhill Farm

DOEHOLE LA   A615

ALDERS LA

Yew Tree
Farm

Cunnery

Dewey Lane Farm

CARR LA

59

CUNNERY LA

Dethick
Common

Moor Wood

HIGH LA

Balk Wood

Wood Lane

Cookhill Plantation

Nursery

1

WOOD LA

Well
Wood

DETHICK LA

Canada
Farm

DEWY LA

CROSS LANES

LITTLEMOOR

SWAN LA

Dethick

58

MILL LA

Babbington Farm

32   A   33   B   34   C

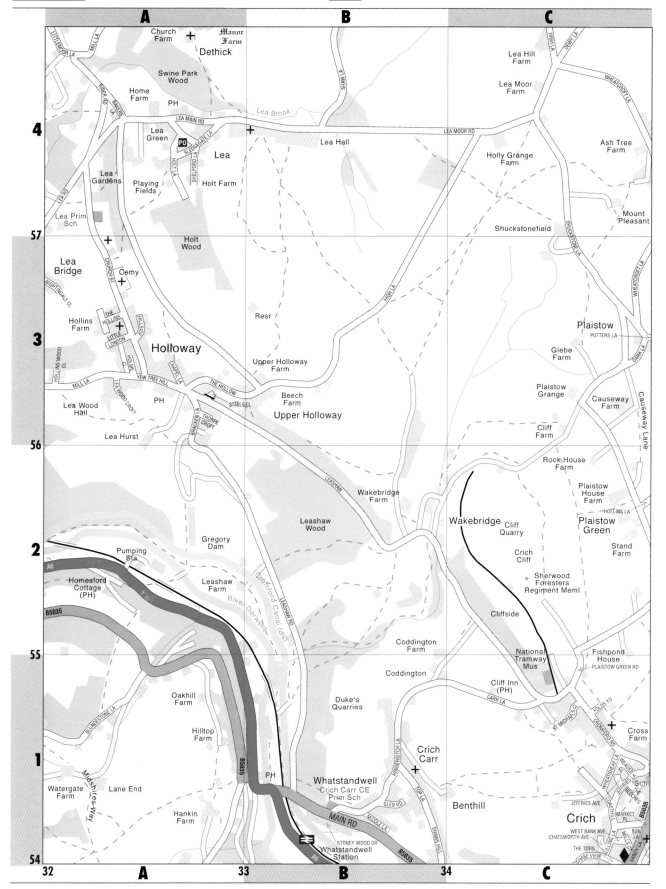

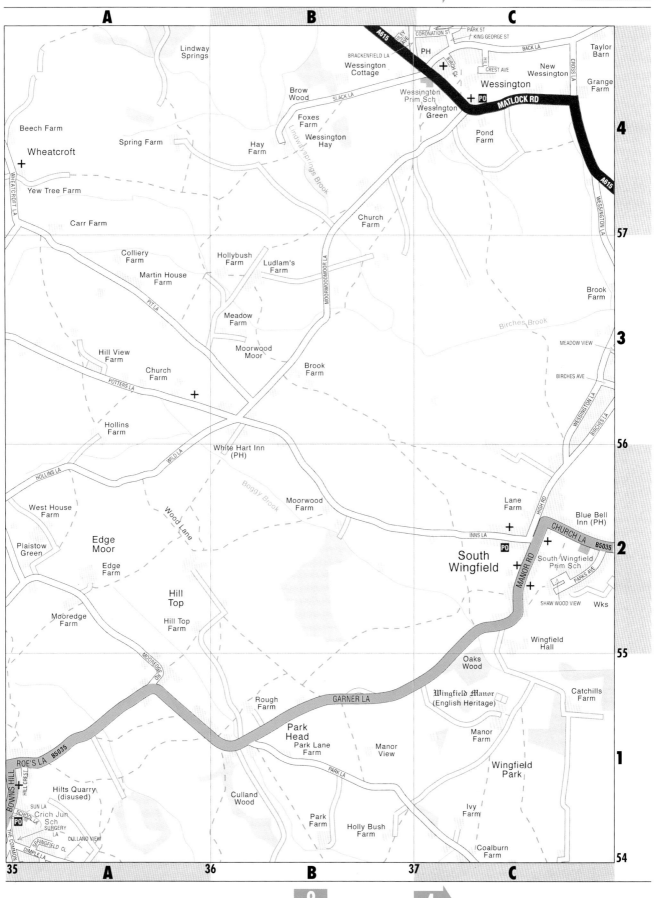

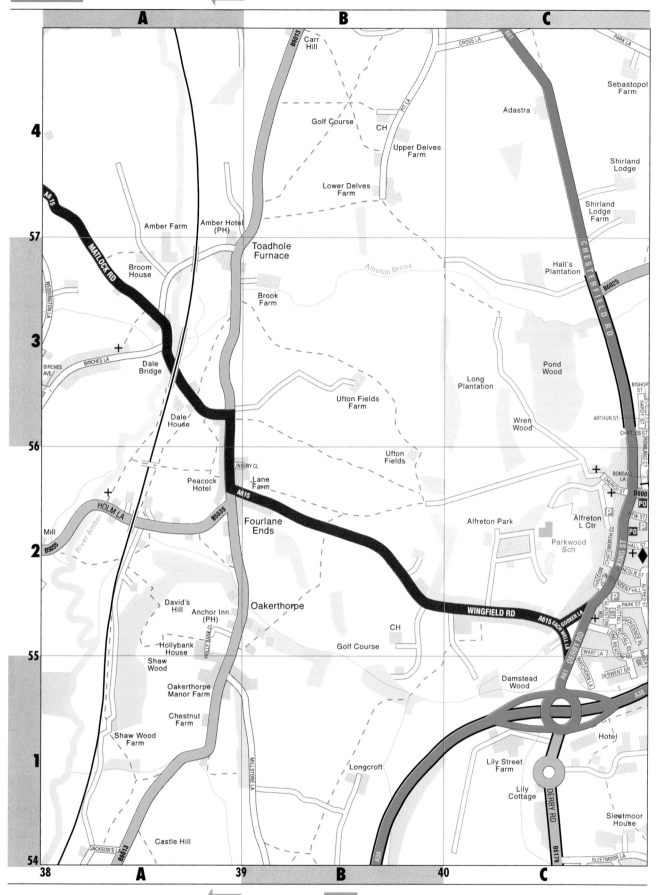

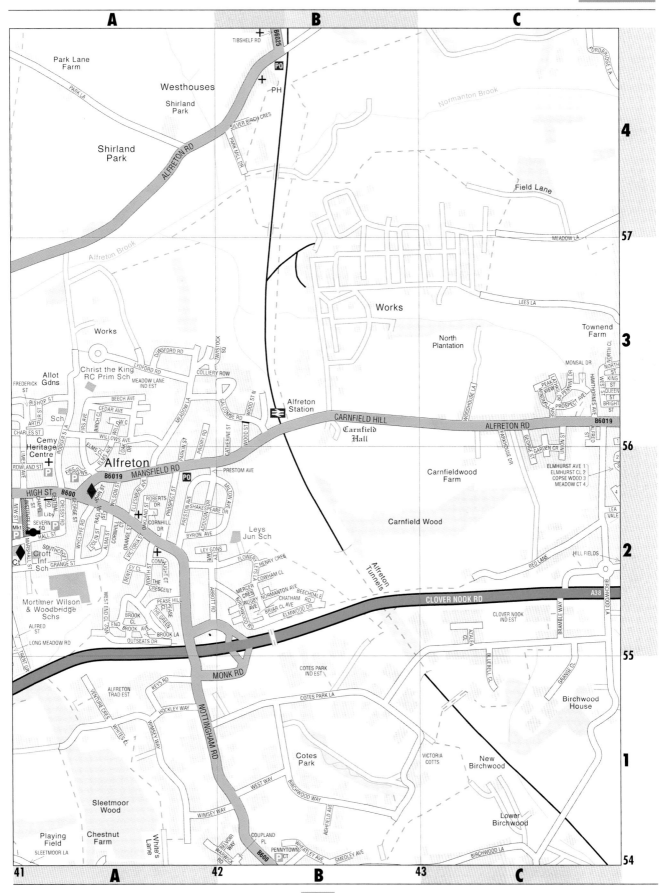

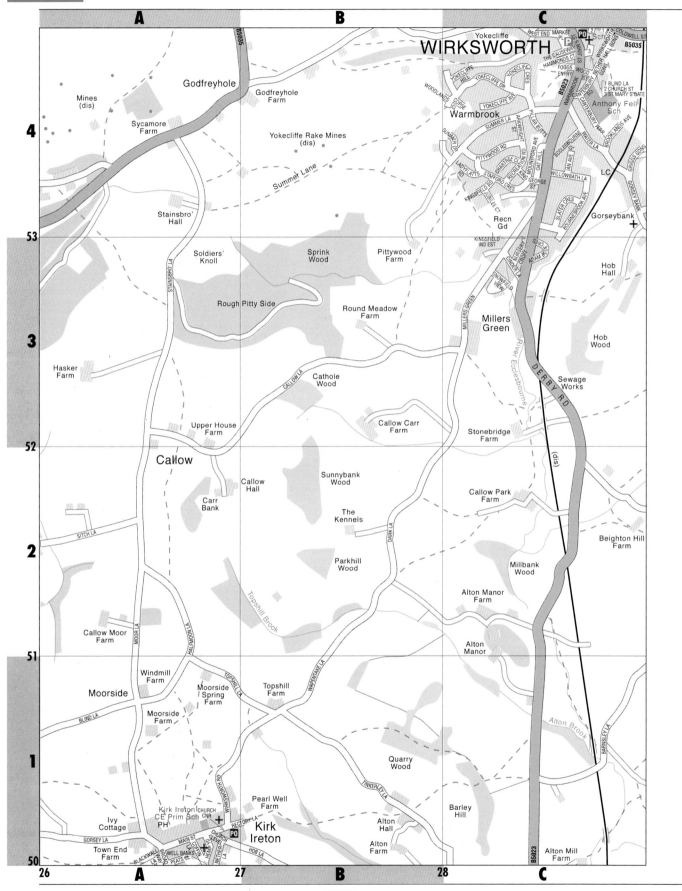

Godfreyhole

Godfreyhole Farm

Mines (dis)

Sycamore Farm

Yokecliffe Rake Mines (dis)

Summer Lane

Stainsbro' Hall

WIRKSWORTH

Yokecliffe

WEST END

MARKET PL

COLDWELL ST

THE CAUSEWAY

HAMMONDS CT

FOGGS ENTRY

1 BLIND LA
2 CHURCH ST
3 ST. MARY'S GATE

B5035

Warmbrook

WOODLANDS COPSE

YOKECLIFFE HILL

YOKECLIFFE DR

YOKECLIFFE CRES

YOKECLIFFE AVE

SUMMER LA

ARKWRIGHT ST

PILLAR BUTTS

CANTERBURY TERR

NETHER HALL GDNS

WOOD

CANTERBURY RD

Anthony Fell Sch

SUMMER DR

PITTYWOOD RD

CRABTREE CL

RECREATION RD

MOUNTFORD AVE

ECCLESBOURNE

IAN AVE

WATER LA

WILLOWBATH LA

BROOKLANDS AVE

GRIGGS GDNS

GORSEY BANK

LC

LADYFLATTS RD

STAFFORD CRES

KING GEORGE ST

KINGSFIELD RD

JUBILEE CT

SLATER CRES

BOURNEBROOK AVE

Gorseybank

Recn Gd

KINGSFIELD IND EST

Soldiers' Knoll

Sprink Wood

Pittywood Farm

NURSERY CROFT

ADAM BEDE

SNOWFIELD VIEW

CINDER LA

Hob Hall

Rough Pitty Side

Round Meadow Farm

Millers Green

MILLERS GREEN

River Ecclesbourne

DERBY RD

Hob Wood

Hasker Farm

CALLOW LA

Cathole Wood

Sewage Works

Upper House Farm

Callow Carr Farm

Stonebridge Farm

(dis)

Callow

Callow Hall

Sunnybank Wood

Callow Park Farm

Beighton Hill Farm

Carr Bank

The Kennels

DARK LA

Millbank Wood

SITCH LA

Parkhill Wood

Alton Manor Farm

Callow Moor Farm

MOOR LA

PALMOOR LA

Topshill Brook

Alton Manor

Alton Brook

BARNSLEY LA

Windmill Farm

TOPSHILL LA

Moorside Spring Farm

Topshill Farm

WAPENTAKE LA

Moorside

BLIND LA

Moorside Farm

Quarry Wood

TINKERLEY LA

Barley Hill

Ivy Cottage

Kirk Ireton CE Prim Sch

CHURCH CNR

PH

WIRKSWORTH RD

RECTORY LA

Pearl Well Farm

Kirk Ireton

Alton Hall

Alton Farm

GORSEY LA

Town End Farm

BLACKWALL LA

MAIN ST

WELL BANKS

PEATS CT

HEMP LA

NETHER LA

CHURCH LA

COFFIN LA

HOB LA

B5023

Alton Mill Farm

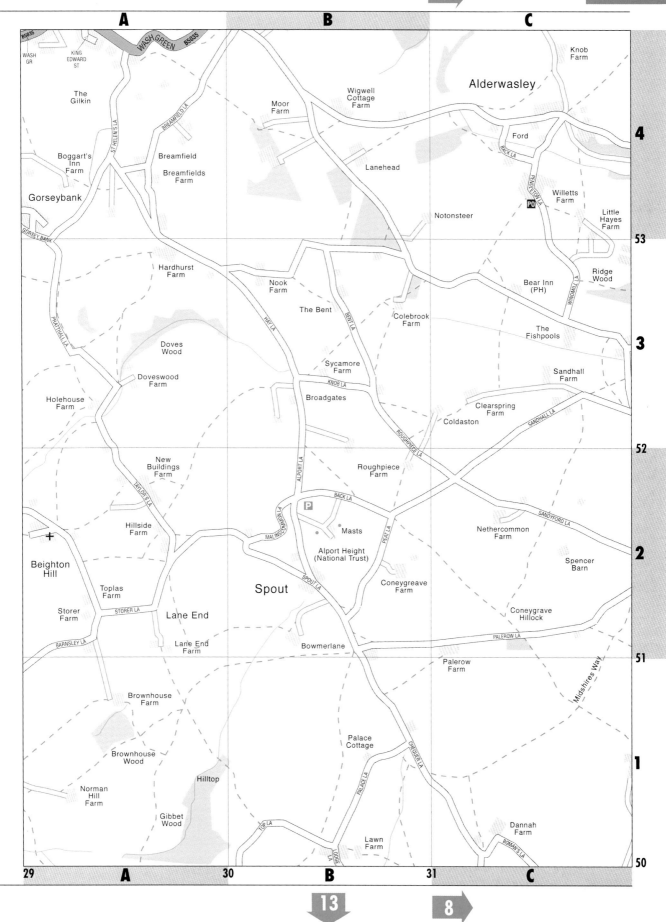

A　　　　　　　　B　　　　　　　　C

B5035

WASH GREEN B5035

WASH GR

KING EDWARD ST

The Gilkin

Moor Farm

Wigwell Cottage Farm

Knob Farm

Alderwasley

Boggart's Inn Farm

Breamfield

Breamfields Farm

BREAMFIELD LA

ST HELEN'S LA

Lanehead

Ford

BACK LA

4

Gorseybank

GORSEY BANK

Notonsteer

PENDLETON LA

PO

Willetts Farm

Little Hayes Farm

53

Hardhurst Farm

PRATTHALL LA

Nook Farm

HAY LA

BENT LA

The Bent

Colebrook Farm

Bear Inn (PH)

WINDMILL LA

Ridge Wood

The Fishpools

3

Doves Wood

Sycamore Farm

Doveswood Farm

KNOB LA

Broadgates

Clearspring Farm

SANDHALL LA

Sandhall Farm

Holehouse Farm

Coldaston

ROUGHPIECE LA

52

New Buildings Farm

TAYLOR'S LA

ALPORT LA

Roughpiece Farm

Coneygreave Farm

SANDYFORD LA

Nethercommon Farm

Spencer Barn

2

Hillside Farm

P

BACK LA

MALINSCOMMON LA

Masts

Alport Height (National Trust)

PEAT LA

Beighton Hill

Toplas Farm

STORER LA

Lane End

SPOUT LA

Spout

Coneygrave Hillock

Storer Farm

BARNSLEY LA

Lane End Farm

Bowmerlane

PALEROW LA

Palerow Farm

Midshires Way

51

Brownhouse Farm

Palace Cottage

PALACE LA

CHEQUER LA

1

Brownhouse Wood

Hilltop

Norman Hill Farm

Gibbet Wood

TOP LA

Lawn Farm

LODGE LA

Dannah Farm

BOMAN'S LA

50

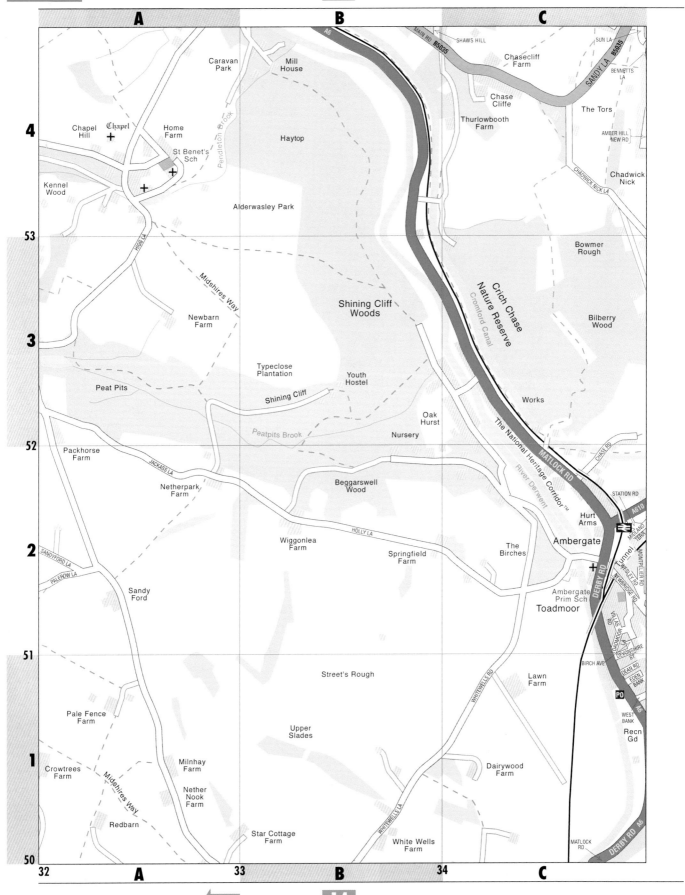

A **B** **C**

Caravan
Park

Mill
House

Chapel Hill · Chapel · Home Farm

Haytop

Shaws Hill

MAIN RD B5035

Chasecliff
Farm

SUN LA

SANDY LA

B5035

BENNETTS
LA

Chase
Cliffe

The Tors

Thurlowbooth
Farm

AMBER HILL
NEW RD

St Benet's
Sch

Kennel
Wood

Pendleton Brook

Alderwasley Park

CHADWICK NICK LA

Chadwick
Nick

4

HIGG LA

53

Midshires Way

Newbarn
Farm

Shining Cliff
Woods

Crich Chase
Nature Reserve

Cromford Canal

Bowmer
Rough

Bilberry
Wood

3

Typeclose
Plantation

Youth
Hostel

Peat Pits

Shining Cliff

Oak
Hurst

Works

The National Heritage Corridor™

Peatpits Brook

Nursery

MATLOCK RD

CHASE RD

52

Packhorse
Farm

JACKASS LA

Netherpark
Farm

Beggarswell
Wood

River Derwent

STATION RD

A610

Hurt
Arms

Ambergate

MIDLAND
TERR

MONTPELIER RD

2

SANDYFORD LA

PALEROW LA

Wiggonlea
Farm

HOLLY LA

Springfield
Farm

The
Birches

Tunnel

DERBY RD

WESLEY RD

NEWBRIDGE RD

Sandy
Ford

Ambergate
Prim Sch

Toadmoor

VILLAS
RD

RADMOOR
RD

DEVONSHIRE
ST

51

Street's Rough

Lawn
Farm

BIRCH AVE

DEAN RD

EDEN
BANK

Pale Fence
Farm

Upper
Slades

WHITEWELLS RD

PO

WEST
BANK

Recn
Gd

1

Crowtrees
Farm

Midshires Way

Milnhay
Farm

Nether
Nook
Farm

Dairywood
Farm

WHITEWELLS LA

DERBY RD A6

Redbarn

Star Cottage
Farm

White Wells
Farm

MATLOCK
RD

MATLOCK RD

DERBY RD   A6

32 **A** **33** **B** **34** **C**

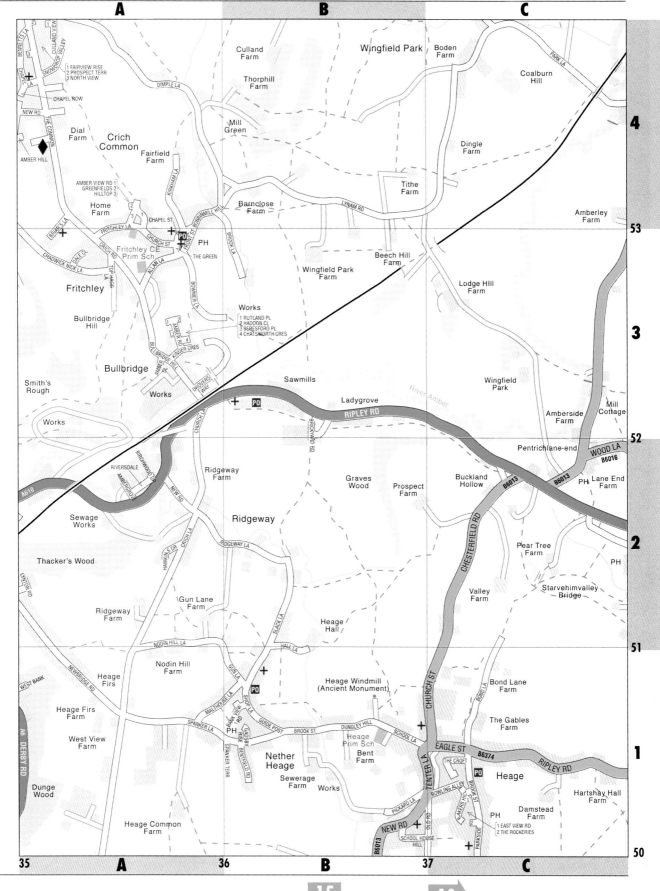

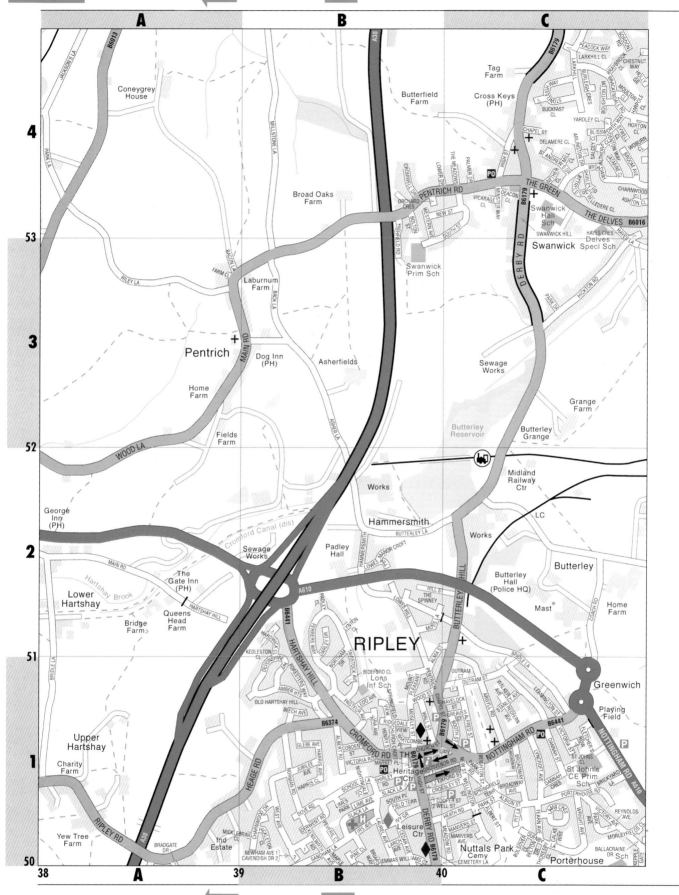

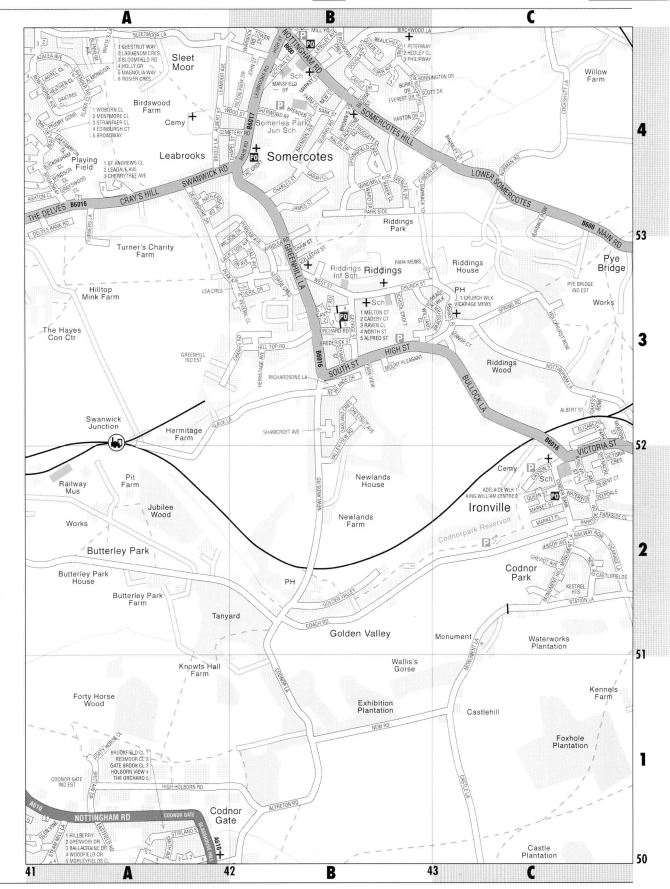

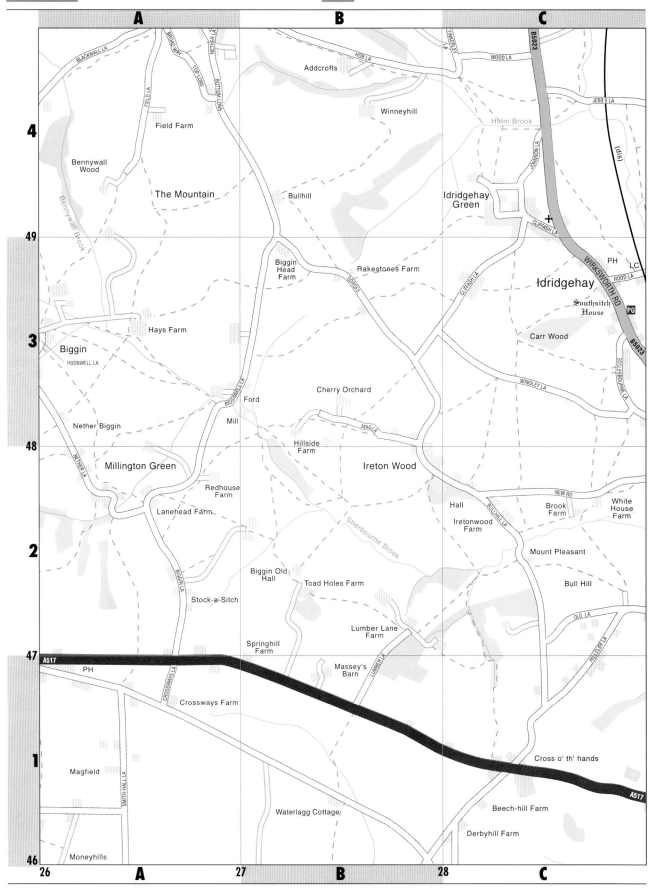

A B C

4

49

3

Biggin

2

47

1

46

26 A 27 B 28 C

BLACKWALL LA
BROAD WAY
NETHER LA
FIELD LA
TOP LONS
BOTTOM LONS
HOB LA
TINKERLEY LA
WOOD LA
B5023
JEBB'S LA
(dis)

Addcrofts

Winneyhill

Field Farm

Holm Brook

Bennywall
Wood

The Mountain

Bullhill

Idridgehay
Green

Bennywall Brook

Biggin
Head
Farm

Rakestones Farm

GORSES

JOHNSON LA

CLIFFASH LA

Idridgehay

Hays Farm

CLIFFASH LA

Carr Wood

Southsitch
House

PH
LC
ROOD LA
WIRKSWORTH RD
PO
B5023

HOONWELL LA

BIGGINMILL LA

Ford

Mill

Cherry Orchard

WINDLEY LA

ECCLESBOURNE LA

Nether Biggin

MAG LA

Hillside
Farm

Ireton Wood

48

Millington Green

NETHER LA

Redhouse
Farm

Lanehead Farm

Sherbourne Brook

Hall

Iretonwood
Farm

BULLHILL LA

NEW RD

Brook
Farm

White
House
Farm

Mount Pleasant

Bull Hill

BIGGIN LA

Stock-a-Sitch

Biggin Old
Hall

Toad Holes Farm

OLD LA

HILLCLIFF LA

Springhill
Farm

Lumber Lane
Farm

LUMBER LA

A517
PH

CROSSWAYS LA

Crossways Farm

Massey's
Barn

Cross o' th' hands

A517

Magfield

SMITH-HALL LA

Waterlagg Cottage

Beech-hill Farm

Derbyhill Farm

Moneyhills

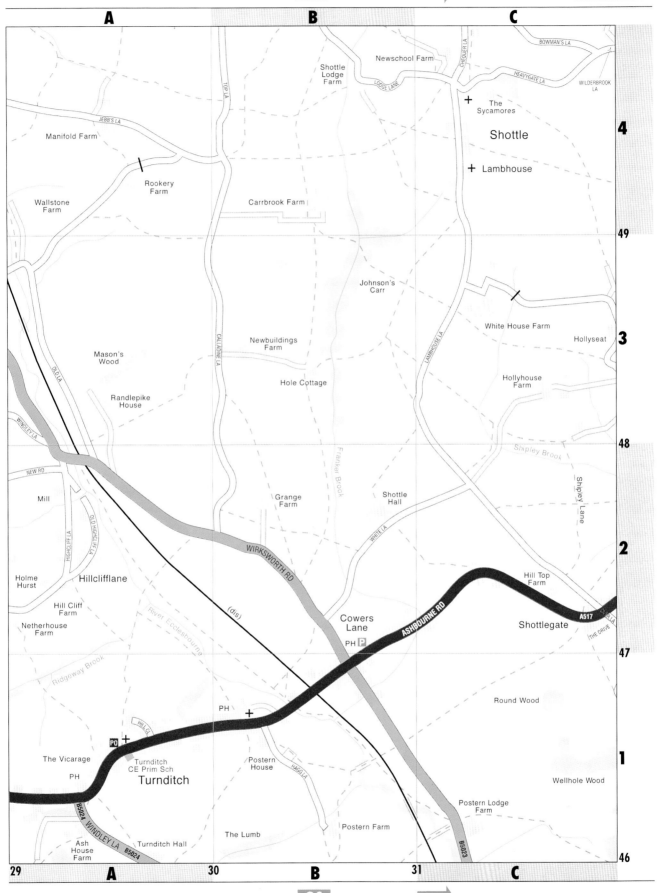

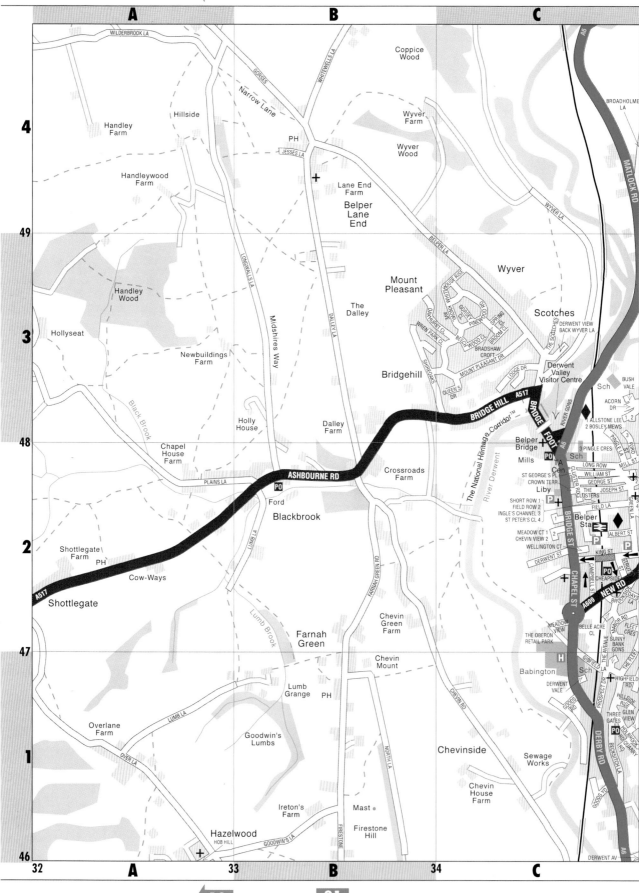

A   B   C

WILDERBROOK LA

4

Handley Farm

Hillside

Handleywood Farm

Narrow Lane

GORSES

WHITEWELLS LA

Coppice Wood

Wyver Farm

Wyver Wood

PH

JESSES LA

Lane End Farm

Belper Lane End

BROADHOLME LA

MATLOCK RD

A6

49

Handley Wood

Hollyseat

Newbuildings Farm

LONGWALLS LA

Midshires Way

DALLEY LA

The Dalley

BELPER LA

Mount Pleasant

Wyver

Scotches

HOUSE RISE

GORSEY CL

KILN WY

PINEWOOD

OLD SPRING

DERWENT VIEW

BACK WYVER LA

WYVER LA

Sch

BUSH VALE

ACORN DR

3

Bridgehill

WREN PARK CL

OAKHURST CL

BEECH

WOOD CL

BROOM CL

BRADSHAW CROFT

SHIRE OAKS

MOUNT PLEASANT DR

QUEEN'S DR

LODGE DR

Derwent Valley Visitor Centre

1 ALLSTONE LEE
2 BOSLEY MEWS

Black Brook

Chapel House Farm

Holly House

Dalley Farm

BRIDGE HILL   A517

BRIDGE FOOT

Belper Bridge

A6

River Derwent

PINGLE LA

FORD ST

MILL ST

48

PLAINS LA

ASHBOURNE RD

PQ

Ford

Crossroads Farm

Belper Mills

PO

The National Heritage Corridor™

St George's Pl

CROWN TERR

LONG ROW

WILLIAM ST

GEORGE ST

THE CLUSTERS

JOSEPH ST

3 PINGLE CRES

Sch

TA Cen

Liby

CLUSTER RD

GREEN LA

Blackbrook

LUMB LA

SHORT ROW 1
FIELD ROW 2
INGLE'S CHANNEL 3
ST PETER'S CL 4

FIELD LA

2

Shottlegate Farm

PH

Cow-Ways

A517

Shottlegate

Lumb Brook

Farnah Green

FARNAH GREEN RD

Chevin Green Farm

MEADOW CT 1
CHEVIN VIEW 2
WELLINGTON CT

DERWENT ST

Belper Sta

ALBERT ST

KING ST

P

P

PO

STRUTT ST

CAMPBELL ST

CHEAPSIDE

BRIDGE ST

CHAPEL ST

A609   NEW RD

BROAD HOLM

BROADWAY

MANOR RD

FLEET CRES

47

Overlane Farm

LUMB LA

OVER LA

Lumb Grange

PH

Goodwin's Lumbs

Chevin Mount

CHEVIN RD

Chevinside

Babington

H

Sch

DERWENT VALE

THE OBERON RETAIL PARK

MEADOW VIEW

BELLE ACRE CL

THE AVENUE

SUNNY BANK GDNS

GIBFIELD DR

HIGHFIELD RD

HILLSIDE RISE

GLEN VIEW

THREE GATES

1

NORTH LA

Ireton's Farm

Mast

Firestone Hill

Chevin House Farm

Sewage Works

GOODS RD

PROSPECT DR

PO

DERBY RD

BRICKSIDE LA

GOODS YD

46

32   A   33   B   34   C

DERWENT AV

A6

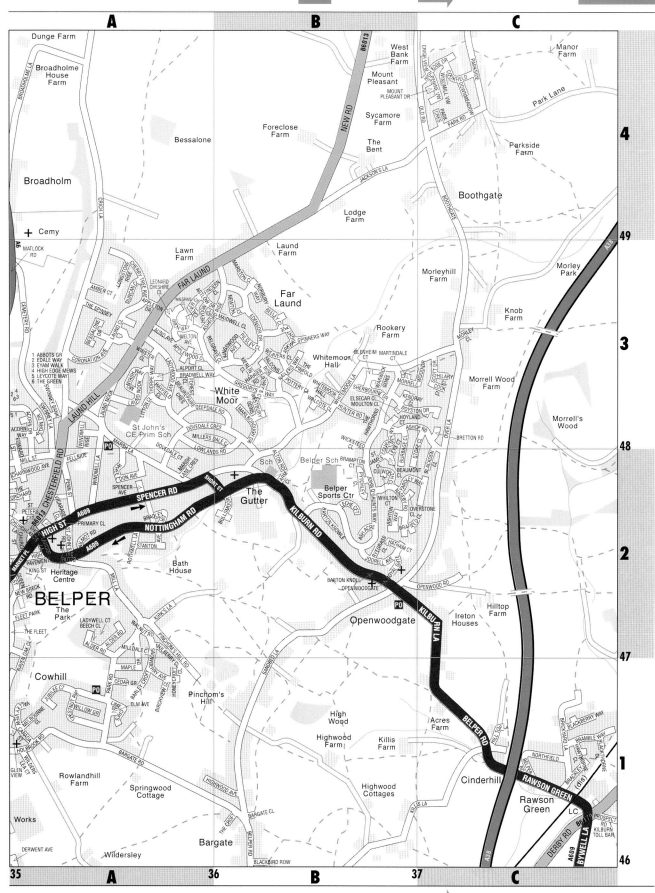

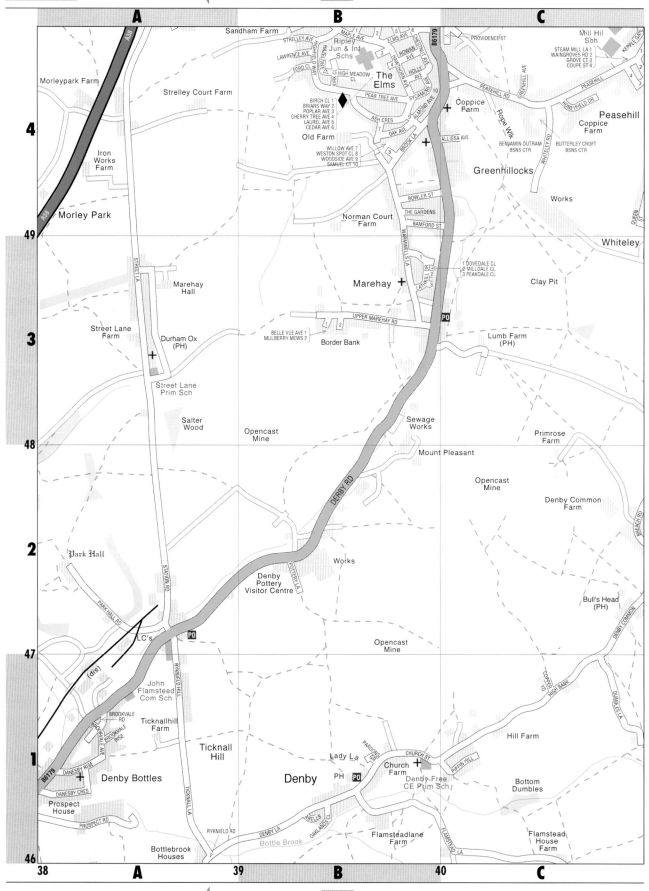

A   B   C

Sandham Farm

Morleypark Farm

Strelley Court Farm

Ripley
Jun & Inf
Schs

Maple Ave
Strelley Ave
Lawrence Ave
Highfield Way
Ford Cl
Hazel Tree
Kirk Cl
High Meadow Cl

Elms Ave
Rowan
Hawthorn Ave
Holly

The
Elms

Providence St

Mill Hil
Sch

Steam Mill La 1
Waingroves Rd 2
Grove Ct 3
Coupe St 4

Kemple Gate

Iron
Works
Farm

Pear Tree Ave

Ash Cres

BIRCH CL 1
BRIARS WAY 2
POPLAR AVE 3
CHERRY TREE AVE 4
LAUREL AVE 5
CEDAR AVE 6

Old Farm

Oak Ave

Almond Ave

Sycamore Ave

Coppice
Farm

Peasehill Rd

Greenfield Ave

Peasehill

Honeyfield Dr

Whiteley Rd

Peasehill
Coppice
Farm

Morley Park

WILLOW AVE 7
WESTON SPOT CL 8
WOODSIDE AVE 9
SAMUEL CT 10

Brook La

Allissa Ave

Benjamin Outram
Bsns Ctr

Butterley Croft
Bsns Ctr

Rope Wlk

Greenhillocks

Works

Queen St

Norman Court
Farm

Bowler St

The Gardens

Bamford St

Whiteley

4

49

Street La

Marehay
Hall

Warmwells La

Marehay

Latykill Dr

1 Dovedale Cl
2 Milldale Cl
3 Peakdale Cl

Clay Pit

Street Lane
Farm

Durham Ox
(PH)

BELLE VUE AVE 1
MULBERRY MEWS 2

Upper Marehay Rd

Border Bank

Lumb Farm
(PH)

3

Street Lane
Prim Sch

PO

Salter
Wood

Opencast
Mine

Sewage
Works

Primrose
Farm

48

Derby Rd

Mount Pleasant

Opencast
Mine

Denby Common
Farm

Beach Rd

2

Park Hall

Park Hall Rd

Station Rd

Pottery La

Works

Denby Pottery
Visitor Centre

Bull's Head
(PH)

Denby Common

LC's

PO

Opencast
Mine

47

(dis)

John
Flamsteed
Com Sch

Ryknield Hill

High Bank

Hill Farm

Dumbles La

Coppice Yd

BROOKVALE
RD

Ticknallhill
Farm

Lady La

Parsons Gn

Church St

Pippin Hill

Brookvale Ave
Brookvale Rise

Ticknall
Hill

PH

PO

Church
Farm

Denby Free
CE Prim Sch

Bottom
Dumbles

1

B6179

Danesby Rise

Denby Bottles

Ticknall La

Denby

Flamsted La

Flamstead
House
Farm

Danesby Cres

Prospect
House

Prospect Rd

Ryknield Rd

Denby La

Abells

Oaklands Cl

Flamsteadlane
Farm

Bottlebrook
Houses

Bottle Brook

46

38   A   39   B   40   C

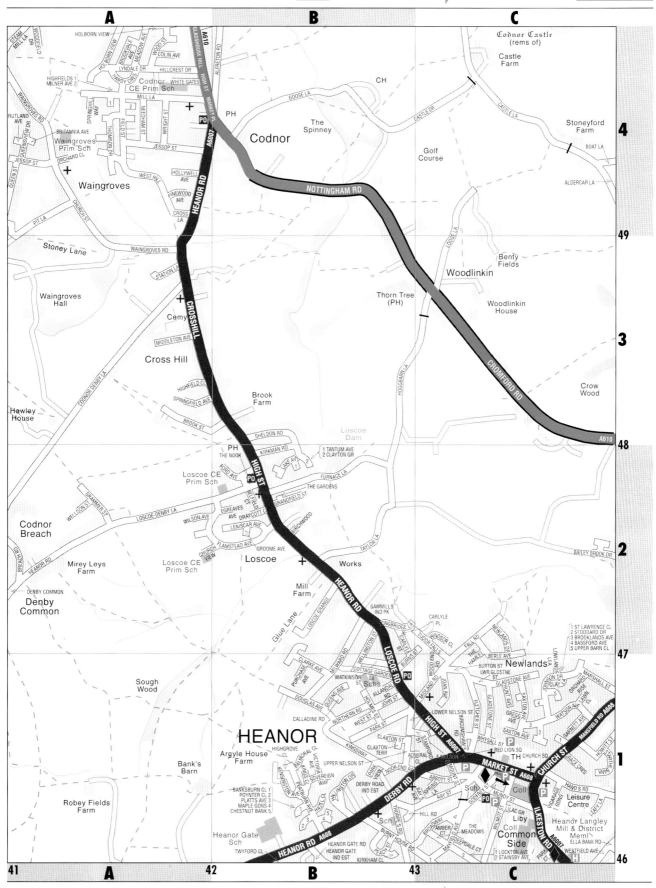

Map labels:

A   B   C

4   49   3   48   2   47   1   46

41   42   43

Codnor area:

STEAM MILL LA
WOODFIELD
HOLBORN VIEW
Codnor Castle (rems of)
Castle Farm
CH
Castle Dr
CASTLE LA
Stoneyford Farm
BOAT LA
ALDERCAR LA
HOLBORN VIEW
BROOKDALE AVE
MEADOW AVE
COLIN AVE
WOOD ST
HILLCREST DR
LYNDALE DR
HARDY CRES
HIGHFIELDS 1
MILNER AVE 2
WHITE GATES
Codnor CE Prim Sch
PH
Codnor
The Spinney
GOOSE LA
CASTLE DR
Golf Course
Woodlinkin
Benty Fields
LOOSE LA
Woodlinkin House
Thorn Tree (PH)
CROMFORD RD
Crow Wood
A610
SPRINGFIELD WAY
THOMSON DR
FIELDS HILL
NEEDHAM ST
WRIGHT ST
JESSOP ST
WEST HILL
HOLLYWELL AVE
PINEWOOD AVE
CROSS HILL
Britannia Ave
Waingroves Prim Sch
RUTLAND AVE
WAINGROVES RD
QUEENSVIEW DR
JESSOP ST
QUEEN ST
ORCHARD CL
Waingroves
PIT LA
CHURCH ST
Stoney Lane
WAINGROVES RD
STATION LA
Waingroves Hall
Cemy
MIDDLETON AVE
Cross Hill
HIGHFIELD CL
SPRINGFIELD AVE
BROOK ST
Brook Farm
SHELDON RD
KIRKMAN RD
Loscoe Dam
1 TANTUM AVE
2 CLAYTON GR
LAKE AVE
FURNACE LA
THE GARDENS
Hawley House
CODNOR DENBY LA
PH
THE NOOK
Loscoe CE Prim Sch
FORD AVE
HIGH ST
PO
BETHFIELD ST
GRANDFIELD ST
GRAMMER ST
WELLDON ST
LOSCOE-DENBY LA
WILSON AVE
EGREAVES AVE
DRAYCOTT CL
BIRCHWOOD
Codnor Breach
LENISCAR AVE
FLAMSTEAD AVE
GROOME AVE
TAYLOR LA
Mirey Leys Farm
BREACH RD
HEANOR RD
Loscoe CE Prim Sch
CHURCH VIEW
Loscoe
Works
HEANOR RD
BAILEY BROOK DR
Denby Common
DENBY COMMON
Mill Farm
SAWMILLS IND PK
CARLYLE PL
1 ST LAWRENCE CL
2 STODDARD DR
3 BROOKLANDS AVE
4 BASSFORD AVE
5 UPPER BARN CL
Glue Lane
LOSCOE GRANGE
LONGBRIDGE LA
TUDOR DR
WINDSOR CL
Newlands
NEWLANDS DR
FALL RD
THE HAMLET
BERLE AVE
LEA
LOWLANDS
Sough Wood
CLARKE AVE
MILWARD RD
WELLINGTON ST
COTTAGE GARDEN LA
BURNS ST
WOOD END RD
BURTON AVE
LWR GLDSTNE
GLADSTONE AVE
JOHNSON DR
CLAY
ORCHARD RISE
MARSHALL ST
PURCHASE AVE
WATKINSON ST
ALLANDALE
MIDLAND RD
JOAN AVE
GLADSTONE ST
GREGG AVE
SAXTON AVE
WATSON AV
LOSCOE RD
PO
DOUGLAS AVE
QUEENS AVE
NORTHERN RD
WEST ST
JOHN ST
PARK ST
Lower Nelson St
FLETCHER RD
WHYSALL ST
GLADSTONE ST
SAXTON AVE
GARNETT AVE
HOWITT ST
HEANOR
CALLADINE RD
HIGHGROVE CL
KINGSWAY
CLAXTON ST
Upper Nelson St
HIGH ST A607
STANFORD ST
BIRCHWOOD RD
Red Lion Sq
TH
CHURCH SQ
MANSFIELD RD A608
CHURCH ST
HAND S RD
GRACE CRES
MARTIN BANK
Argyle House Farm
BALMORAL CL
VICTORIA AVE
KINGS CL
SOVEREIGN WAY
CLAXTON ST
NOOK RD
ADMIRAL CL
EARL SON
Market St A608
P
P
P
Leisure Centre
Bank's Barn
BANKSBURN CL 1
POYNTER CL 2
PLATTS AVE 3
MAPLE GDNS 4
CHESTNUT BANK 5
PEATBURN AVE
WELLINGTON CL
HALL CL
Derby Road Ind Est
DERBY RD
SPRING
RAY ST
Sch
GOODALE ST
PO
MUNDY ST
LILAC GR
Coll
VICARAGE RD
LERET LA
Heanor Langley Mill & District Meml
Robey Fields Farm
Heanor Gate Sch
TWYFORD CL
HEANOR RD A608
Heanor Gate Ind Est
HEANOR GATE RD
KIRKHAM LA
BURNT HOUSE RD
BROADWAY
THORPES RD
HILL RD
AMBER CT
THE MEADOWS
DEEPDALE CT
WEDGEWOOD
MUNDY ST
Liby
Coll
Common Side
1 LOCKTON AVE
2 STAINSBY AVE
ILKESTON RD A607
ELLA BANK RD
WESTFIELD AVE
H

NOTTINGHAM RD

HOGSBROOK LA

HEANOR RD

A610

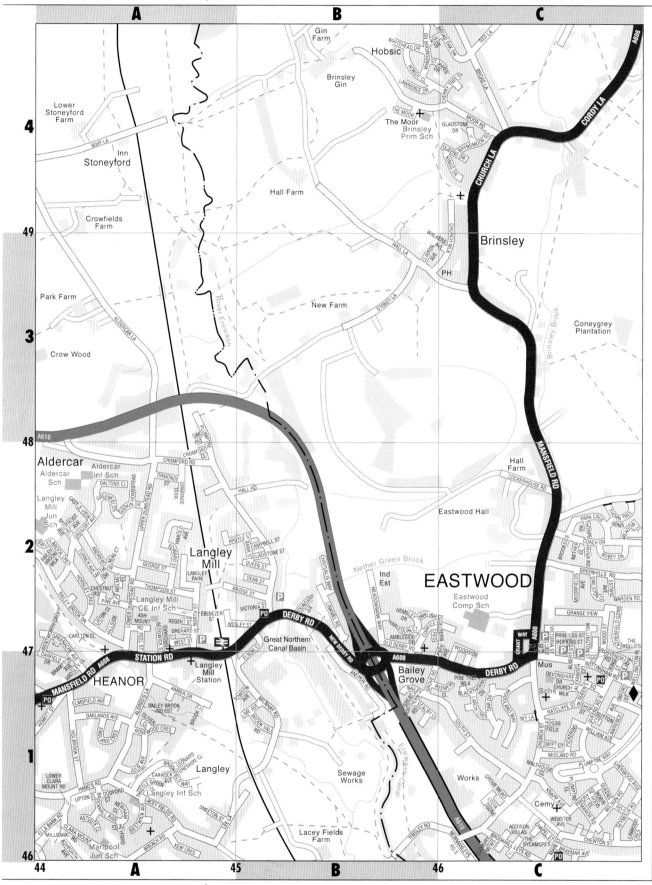

4

49

3

48

2

47

1

46

Hobsic

Gin
Farm

Brinsley
Gin

The Moor
Brinsley
Prim Sch

Lower
Stoneyford
Farm

Inn
Stoneyford

Hall Farm

Brinsley

PH

Crowfields
Farm

Park Farm

New Farm

Coneygrey
Plantation

Crow Wood

Aldercar

Aldercar
Sch

Aldercar
Inf Sch

Langley
Mill
Jun
Sch

Langley
Mill

Langley
Park

Langley Mill
CE Inf Sch

EASTWOOD

Eastwood Hall

Eastwood
Comp Sch

Ind
Est

Hall
Farm

Nether Green Brook

Great Northern
Canal Basin

HEANOR

Langley Mill
Station

Bailey
Grove

Langley

Langley Inf Sch

Sewage
Works

Works

Lacey Fields
Farm

Marlpool
Jun Sch

Cemy

DERBY RD

STATION RD

MANSFIELD RD
A608

CHURCH LA

CORDY LA

A608

MANSFIELD RD

A610

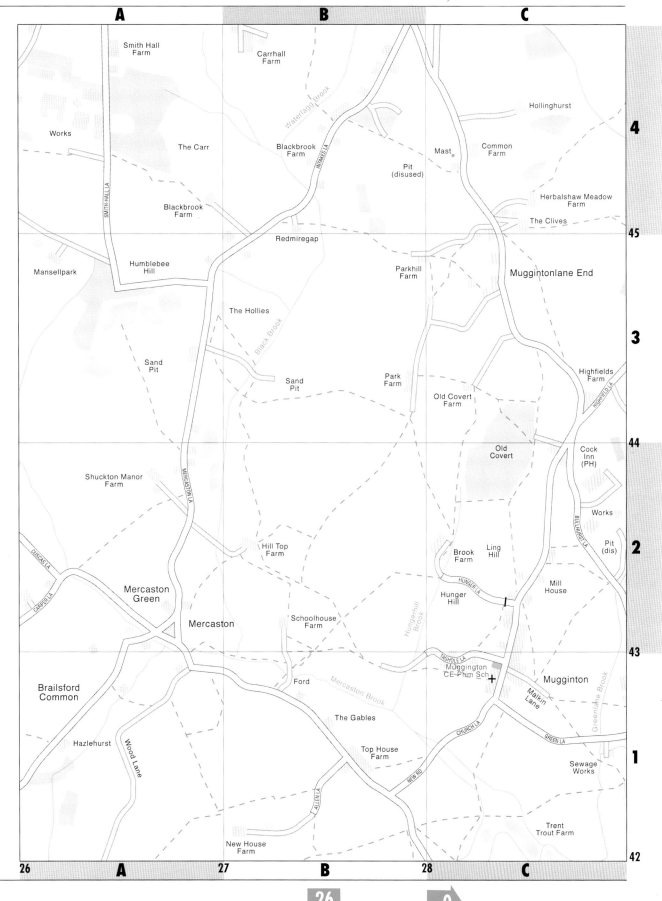

4

Smith Hall
Farm

Carrhall
Farm

Hollinghurst

Works

The Carr

Blackbrook
Farm

Mast

Common
Farm

Pit
(disused)

Herbalshaw Meadow
Farm

SMITH HALL LA

INTAKES LA

Blackbrook
Farm

The Clives

45

Redmiregap

Mansellpark

Humblebee
Hill

Parkhill
Farm

Muggintonlane End

The Hollies

Black Brook

3

Sand
Pit

Sand
Pit

Park
Farm

Old Covert
Farm

Highfields
Farm

HIGHFIELD LA

MERCASTON LA

Old
Covert

44

Shuckton Manor
Farm

Cock
Inn
(PH)

Works

BULLHURST LA

Pit
(dis)

2

Hill Top
Farm

Brook
Farm

Ling
Hill

Mill
House

CUSCAS LA

HUNGER LA

Mercaston
Green

Hunger
Hill

CARPER LA

Mercaston

Schoolhouse
Farm

Hungerhill Brook

43

TAGHOLE LA

Muggington
CE Prim Sch

Mugginton

Brailsford
Common

Ford

Mercaston Brook

Malkin
Lane

Greenlane Brook

The Gables

CHURCH LA

GREEN LA

Hazlehurst

Wood Lane

Top House
Farm

NEW RD

Sewage
Works

1

ALLEN LA

Trent
Trout Farm

New House
Farm

42

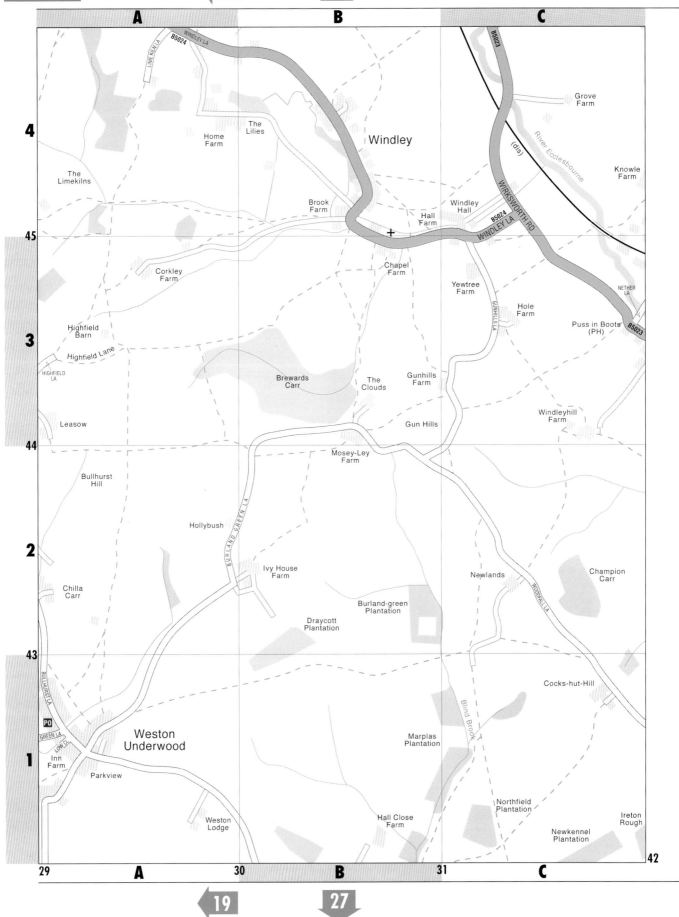

A B C

4

The Limekilns

Home Farm

The Lilies

Windley

B5024 WINDLEY LA

LIME KILN LA

B5023

Grove Farm

River Ecclesbourne

(dis)

Knowle Farm

45

Brook Farm

Hall Farm

Windley Hall

WINDLEY LA

WIRKSWORTH RD

B5024

+

Corkley Farm

Chapel Farm

Yewtree Farm

Hole Farm

GUNHILLS LA

NETHER LA

Puss in Boots (PH)

B5023

3

Highfield Barn

Highfield Lane

HIGHFIELD LA

Brewards Carr

The Clouds

Gunhills Farm

Windleyhill Farm

Leasow

Gun Hills

44

Bullhurst Hill

Mosey-Ley Farm

BURLAND GREEN LA

Hollybush

2

Newlands

WOODFALL LA

Champion Carr

Chilla Carr

Ivy House Farm

Burland-green Plantation

Draycott Plantation

43

Cocks-hut-Hill

BULLHURST LA

PO

GREEN LA

LOW CL

Weston Underwood

Marplas Plantation

Blind Brook

1

Inn Farm

Parkview

Weston Lodge

Hall Close Farm

Northfield Plantation

Newkennel Plantation

Ireton Rough

42

29 A 30 B 31 C

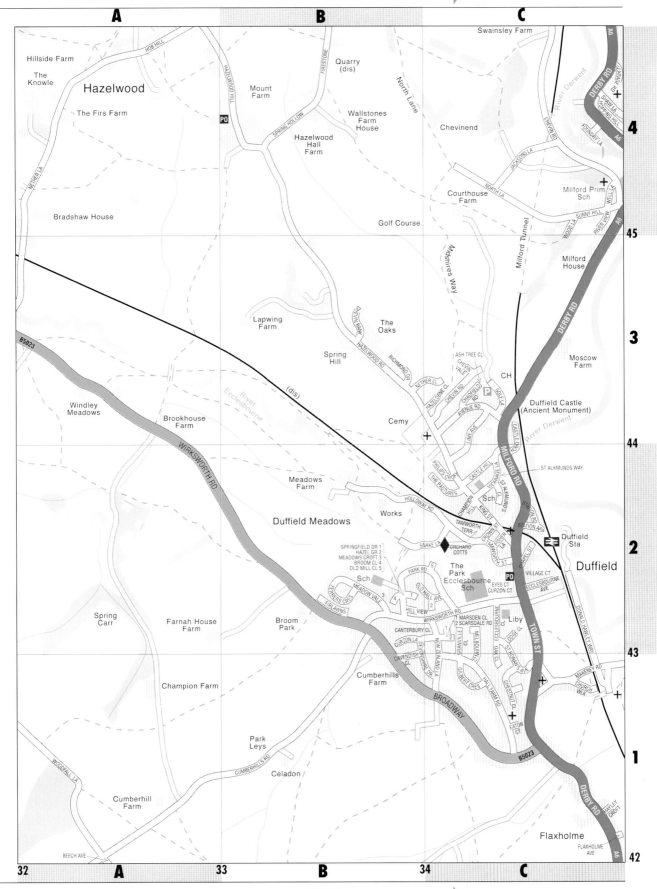

A
B
C

Swainsley Farm

Hillside Farm

The Knowle

Hazelwood

HOB HILL

Mount Farm

Quarry (dis)

FIRESTONE

HAZELWOOD HILL

SPRING HOLLOW

Wallstones Farm House

North Lane

Chevinend

River Derwent

ACREAGE RD

A6

SHAW LA

HOPPING HILL

FOUNDRY LA

A6

The Firs Farm

PO

Hazelwood Hall Farm

JACKSONS LA

Milford Prim Sch

WELL LA

4

NETHER LA

Courthouse Farm

NORTH LA

Bradshaw House

Golf Course

SUNNY HILL

WOOD LA

RIVER VIEW

A6

45

Midshires Way

Milford Tunnel

Milford House

B5023

Lapwing Farm

CHEVIN BANK

HAZELWOOD RD

RICHMOND DR

The Oaks

DERBY RD

Moscow Farm

3

Spring Hill

River Ecclesbourne

(dis)

NETHER CL

ASH TREE CL

CHEVIN VALE

CH

Duffield Castle (Ancient Monument)

River Derwent

Windley Meadows

WIRKSWORTH RD

Brookhouse Farm

Cemy

HAZELDENE CL

CHEVIN RD

CHADFIELD RD

AVENUE RD

P

CASTLE CROFT

SOLE LA

LIME AVE

44

Meadows Farm

PHILLIPS CROFT

THE PASTURES

CASTLE HILL

MILFORD RD

ST ALKMUNDS WAY

Duffield Meadows

Works

HOLLOWAY RD

RICHARD ST

ST ALKMUNDS

CHAPEL HILL

KING ST

Sch

STATION APP

STATION RD

Duffield Sta

2

Duffield

TAMWORTH TERR

SPRINGFIELD DR 1
HAZEL GR 2
MEADOWS CROFT 3
BROOM CL 4
OLD MILL CL 5

SNAKE LA

ORCHARD COTTS

CROWN ST

TAMWORTH ST

FISHER ST

CHAPEL ST

The Park

Ecclesbourne Sch

PO

EYES CT
CURZON CT

VILLAGE CT

ECCLESBOURNE AVE

DONALD HAWLEY WAY

Sch

PARK RD

OLD HALL AVE

MEADOW VALE

3

4

HILL VIEW

WIRKSWORTH RD

MARSDEN CL 1
SCARSDALE RD 2

Liby

TOWN ST

FERRERS CRES

Spring Carr

Farnah House Farm

FIR LAWNS

Broom Park

CURZON LA

DEVONSHIRE DR

NEW ZEALAND LA

CANTERBURY CL

GRANVILLE CL

MELBOURN CL

ECCLESBOURNE CL

LODGE CL

ST ROMAN'S AVE

OAK CL

MAKENEY RD

CHURCH WLK

43

Champion Farm

CAVENDISH CL

Cumberhills Farm

GILBERT CRES

CHESTNUT CL

HALL FARM RD

BROADWAY

B5023

EATON CT

Park Leys

DERBY RD

HAYLEY CROFT

Celadon

CUMBERHILLS RD

WOODFALL LA

Cumberhill Farm

Flaxholme

FLAXHOLME AVE

A6

BEECH AVE

42

32
A
33
B
34
C

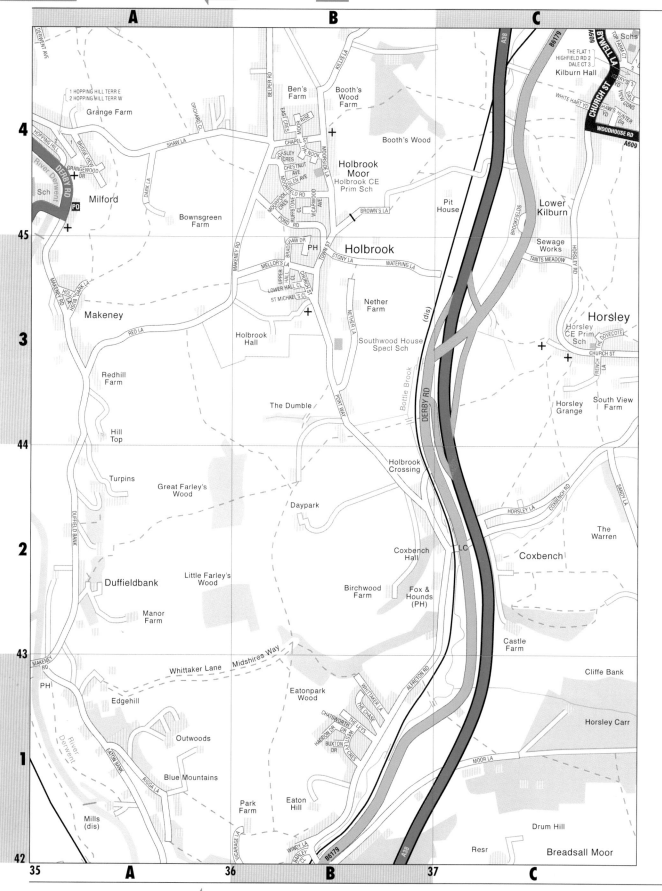

DERWENT AVE
1 HOPPING HILL TERR E
2 HOPPING HILL TERR W
Grange Farm
ORCHARD CL
SHAW LA
HOPPING HILL
River Derwent
DERBY RD
GRANGEWOOD DR
Sch
PO
Milford
BRIDGE VIEW
DARK LA
Bownsgreen Farm

4

BELPER RD
KILL'S LA
Ben's Farm
Booth's Wood Farm
EAST CRES
MOOR RISE
CHAPEL ST
THE NOOK LA
Booth's Wood
UPSLEY CRES
CHESTNUT AVE
GLEN AVE
MOORSIDE LA
Holbrook Moor
Holbrook CE Prim Sch
MOORFIELD RD
MOORDOWN CL
VICARWOOD AVE
POND RD
RUFFSTONE CL
BROWN'S LA
Pit House

45

MAKENEY RD
MELLOR'S LA
UPPER HALL CL
BRADSHAW DR
LOWER HALL CL
CHURCH ST
St MICHAEL'S CL
PH
TOWN ST
STONY LA
Holbrook
WATERING LA
Sewage Works
TANTS MEADOW
Lower Kilburn
BROOKFIELDS
HORSLEY RD

MAKENEY RD
HOLL BUSH LA
DARK LA
Makeney
RED LA
Holbrook Hall
NETHER LA
Nether Farm
Southwood House Specl Sch
(dis)
Horsley
Horsley CE Prim Sch
THE DOVECOTE
CHURCH ST
FRENCH LA

3

Redhill Farm
DUFFIELD BANK
PORT WAY
Bottle Brook
DERBY RD
Horsley Grange
South View Farm

Hill Top
The Dumble

44

Turpins
Great Farley's Wood
Daypark
Holbrook Crossing
HORSLEY LA
COXBENCH RD
The Warren
SANDY LA

2

Little Farley's Wood
Coxbench Hall
LC
Coxbench

Duffieldbank
Birchwood Farm
Fox & Hounds (PH)

Manor Farm
Castle Farm
Cliffe Bank

43

MAKENEY RD
PH
Whittaker Lane
Midshires Way
WHITTAKER LA
ALFRETON RD
Horsley Carr

Edgehill
Eatonpark Wood
THE CHASE
THE LEYS
CHATSWORTH DR
HADDON DR
BUXTON DR
WHEATLEY CRES

River Derwent
EATON BANK
RIGGA LA
Outwoods
Blue Mountains
MOOR LA
Drum Hill

1

Park Farm
Eaton Hill

Mills (dis)
VICARAGE LA
WINDY LA
BARLEY CL
B6179
A38
Resr
Breadsall Moor

42

THE FLAT 1
HIGHFIELD RD 2
DALE CT 3
Kilburn Hall
WHITE HART YD
BYNELL LA
B6179
A609
CHURCH ST
KERRY ST 3
DALE
VIEW GDNS
HUNTER DR
SHAW'S YD
WOODHOUSE RD
A609
TOP FARM CT
Schs

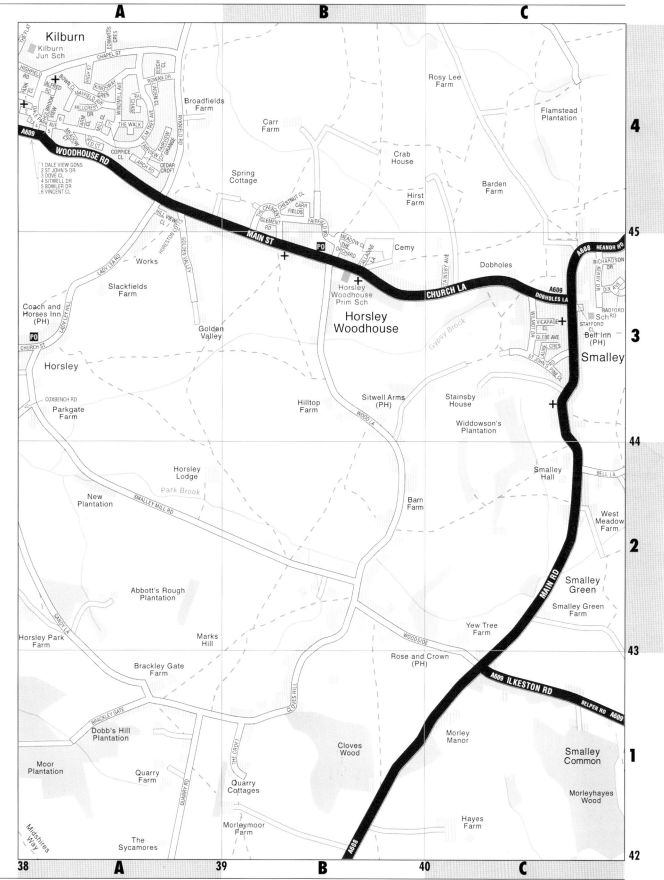

A B C

4

45

3

Kilburn
Kilburn Jun Sch
THE FLAT
EDWARDS CRES
CHAPEL ST
HIGH ST
HIGHFIELD RD
PARK RD
ALFRED CL
HOLBROOK VIEW
BOWN CL
KINGSWAY
MAYFIELD AVE
BEECH CL
ROWAN DR
THE CHASE
DALE PARK AVE
MEADOW
HILLCREST
WINDMILL AVE
ELM TREE AVE
FAIRVIEW CL
RYKNIELD RD
FIELD CT
PARK
FARM CL
THE WALK
GRANGE
COPPICE CL
LARCH CL
CEDAR CROFT
FAIRVIEW CL
A609
WOODHOUSE RD

1 DALE VIEW GDNS
2 ST JOHN'S DR
3 DOVE CL
4 SITWELL DR
5 BOWLER DR
6 VINCENT CL

Broadfields Farm

Spring Cottage

Carr Farm

Rosy Lee Farm

Flamstead Plantation

Crab House

Barden Farm

Hirst Farm

HILL VIEWS CL
HORESTON RD
GOLDEN VALLEY
LADY LEA RD
MAIN ST
THE CRES
CHESTNUT CL
CLEMENT RD
CARR FIELDS
FAIRFIELD RD
MEADOW CL
THE ORCHARD
TALLANBE LA
PO

Works

Cemy

Dobholes

A608 HEANOR RD
RICHARDSON DR
KERRY DR
DIX AVE
RADFORD RD
STAFFORD CL

Slackfields Farm

Horsley Woodhouse Prim Sch

CHURCH LA

STAINSBY AVE

A609

DOBHOLES LA

VICARAGE CL
WILMOT DR
GLEBE AVE
LAUREL CRES
ST JOHN'S RD
PINE CL

Bell Inn (PH)

Smalley

Coach and Horses Inn (PH)

LADY LEY HILL

Golden Valley

Horsley Woodhouse

Gypsy Brook

PO
CHURCH ST

Horsley

Sitwell Arms (PH)

Stainsby House

Widdowson's Plantation

COXBENCH RD

Parkgate Farm

Hilltop Farm

WOOD LA

44

Horsley Lodge

Park Brook

SMALLEY MILL RD

Barn Farm

Smalley Hall

BELL LA

New Plantation

West Meadow Farm

2

Abbott's Rough Plantation

MAIN RD

Smalley Green

Smalley Green Farm

SANDY LA

Horsley Park Farm

Marks Hill

WOODSIDE

Yew Tree Farm

43

Brackley Gate Farm

Rose and Crown (PH)

A609 ILKESTON RD

BELPER RD A609

BRACKLEY GATE

CLOVES HILL

Dobb's Hill Plantation

THE CROFT

Cloves Wood

Morley Manor

Smalley Common

1

Moor Plantation

Quarry Farm

QUARRY RD

Quarry Cottages

Morleyhayes Wood

Midshires Way

The Sycamores

Morleymoor Farm

A608

Hayes Farm

42

38 A 39 B 40 C

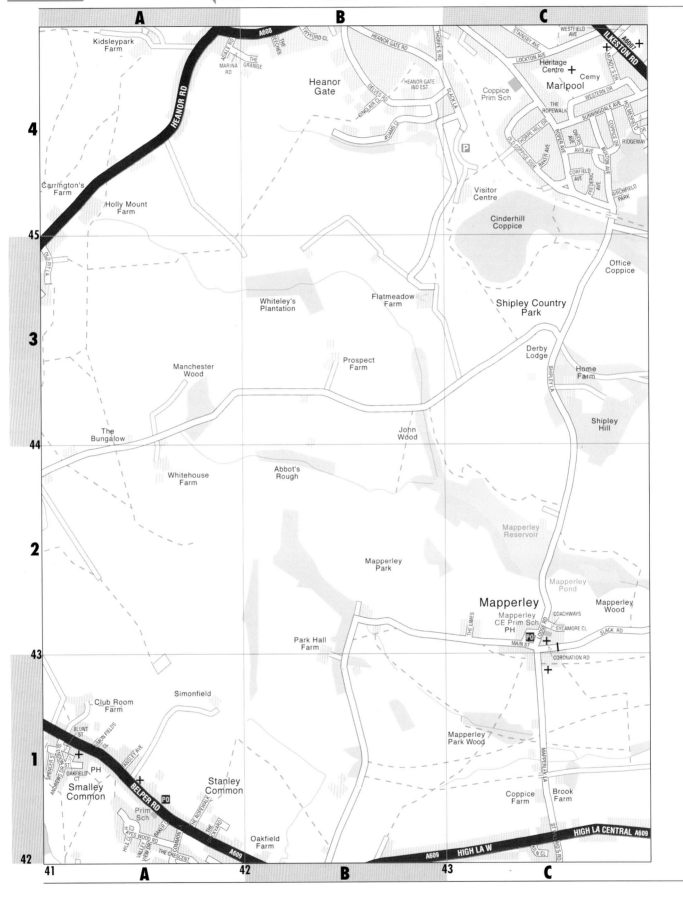

A **B** **C**

Kidsleypark Farm

THE BEECHES

TWYFORD CL

HEANOR GATE RD

THORPE'S RD

WESTFIELD AVE

STAINSBY AVE

LOCKTON AVE

MINDY'S DR

ILKESTON RD

A6007

AGALE RD

MARINA RD

THE GRANGE

A608

DELVES RD

SINCLAIR CL

HEANOR GATE IND EST

Heritage Centre

Cemy

Marlpool

HEANOR RD

Heanor Gate

ADAMS CL

SLACK LA

Coppice Prim Sch

THE ROPEWALK

WESTERN DR

SUNNINGDALE AVE

HOLMESFIELD DR

COPPICE DR

OLD THORPE HILL

ROPER AVE

OWERS AVE

AVIS AVE

BUXTON AVE

Ridgeway

4

Carrington's Farm

Holly Mount Farm

P

Visitor Centre

BAKER AVE

CORFIELD AVE

FREDERIC AVE

BIRCHFIELD PARK

45

OLD PIT LA

Cinderhill Coppice

Office Coppice

Whiteley's Plantation

Flatmeadow Farm

Shipley Country Park

3

Manchester Wood

Prospect Farm

Derby Lodge

SHIPLEY LA

Home Farm

The Bungalow

John Wood

Shipley Hill

44

Whitehouse Farm

Abbot's Rough

Mapperley Reservoir

2

Mapperley Park

Mapperley Pond

Mapperley Wood

Mapperley

THE LIMES

Mapperley CE Prim Sch

PH

COACHWAYS

SYCAMORE CL

ROSE RD

PO

SLACK RD

Park Hall Farm

MAIN ST

CORONATION RD

43

Club Room Farm

Simonfield

BLUNT ST

SPENCER ST

ANDREWS DR

WOODS RD

SIMON FIELDS CL

TANSLEY AVE

OAKFIELD CT

PH

Mapperley Park Wood

MAPPERLEY LA

1

Smalley Common

BELPER RD

PO

Stanley Common

Coppice Farm

Brook Farm

ST HILDA'S RD

HILL CL

HAYES WOOD RD

VALLEY VIEW DR

THE ROPEWALK

THE BLAZARD

Prim Sch

THE COMMON

THE CRESCENT

Oakfield Farm

A609

HIGH LA W

KILN CL

HIGH LA CENTRAL A609

42

41 **A** **42** **B** **43** **C**

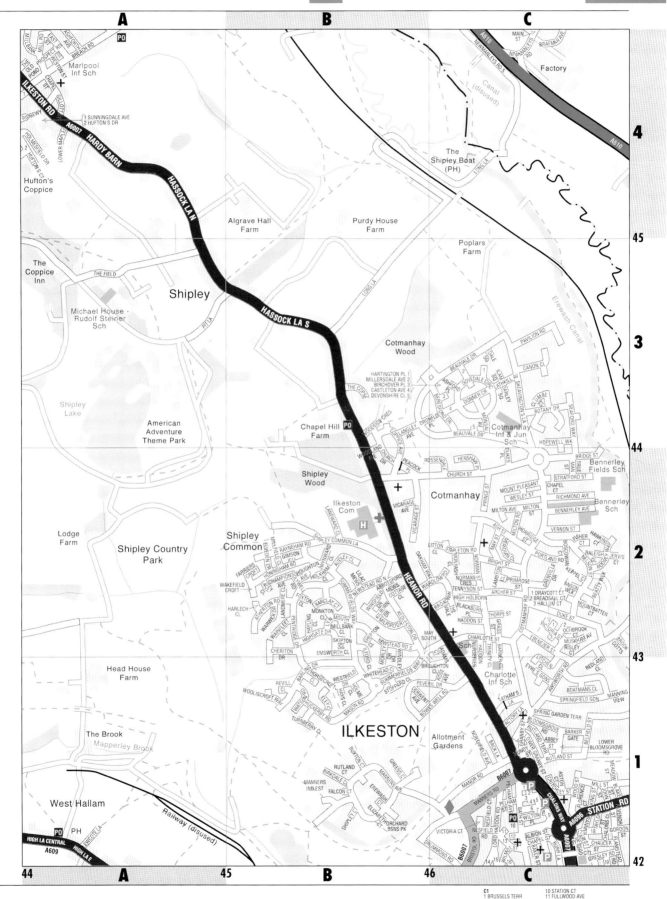

C1
1 BRUSSELS TERR
2 BURLEIGH ST
3 STAMFORD ST
4 ESSEX ST
5 DURHAM ST
6 NORTHGATE ST
7 WILTON ST
8 WEST TERR
9 NORTH ST
10 STATION CT
11 FULLWOOD AVE
12 PROVIDENCE PL
13 FULLWOOD ST
14 WHARNCLIFFE RD
15 JACKSON AVE
16 GREGORY ST
17 CHAPEL ST
18 LOWER CHAPEL ST
19 RIGLEY AVE

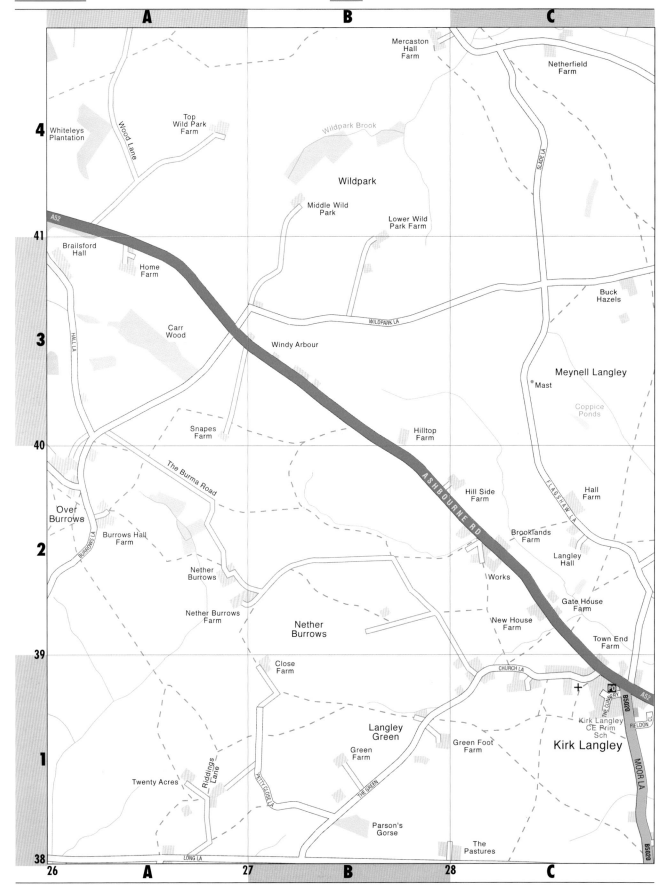

Mercaston Hall Farm

Netherfield Farm

4 Whiteleys Plantation

Top Wild Park Farm

Wood Lane

Wildpark Brook

SLADE LA

Wildpark

Middle Wild Park

Lower Wild Park Farm

41

A52

Brailsford Hall

Home Farm

Buck Hazels

HALL LA

Carr Wood

WILDPARK LA

3 Windy Arbour

Meynell Langley

Mast

Coppice Ponds

Snapes Farm

Hilltop Farm

40

The Burma Road

Hill Side Farm

FLAGSHAW LA

Hall Farm

Over Burrows

ASHBOURNE RD

Burrows Hall Farm

BURROWS LA

BrookIands Farm

2

Langley Hall

Nether Burrows

Works

Gate House Farm

Nether Burrows Farm

Nether Burrows

New House Farm

Town End Farm

39

Close Farm

CHURCH LA

PO

B5020

THE GLUMERY

Kirk Langley CE Prim Sch

FIELDON

Langley Green

1

Green Farm

Green Foot Farm

Kirk Langley

Twenty Acres

Riddings Lane

THE GREEN

MOOR LA

PETTY CLOSE LA

Parson's Gorse

The Pastures

38

LONG LA

B5020

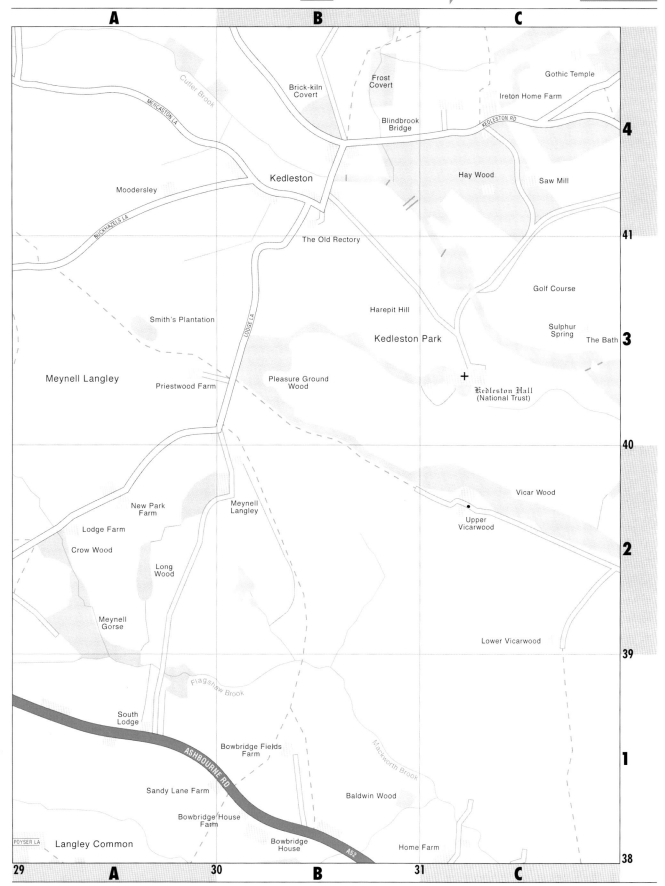

A   B   C

Brick-kiln Covert

Frost Covert

Gothic Temple

Ireton Home Farm

Blindbrook Bridge

KEDLESTON RD

Kedleston

Hay Wood

Saw Mill

Moodersley

MERCASTON LA

Cutter Brook

BUCKHAZELS LA

The Old Rectory

Golf Course

Harepit Hill

Smith's Plantation

LODGE LA

Kedleston Park

Sulphur Spring

The Bath

Meynell Langley

Priestwood Farm

Pleasure Ground Wood

+ Kedleston Hall (National Trust)

Vicar Wood

New Park Farm

Meynell Langley

• Upper Vicarwood

Lodge Farm

Crow Wood

Long Wood

Meynell Gorse

Lower Vicarwood

Flagshaw Brook

South Lodge

ASHBOURNE RD

Bowbridge Fields Farm

Mackworth Brook

Sandy Lane Farm

Baldwin Wood

Bowbridge House Farm

POYSER LA

Langley Common

Bowbridge House

A52

Home Farm

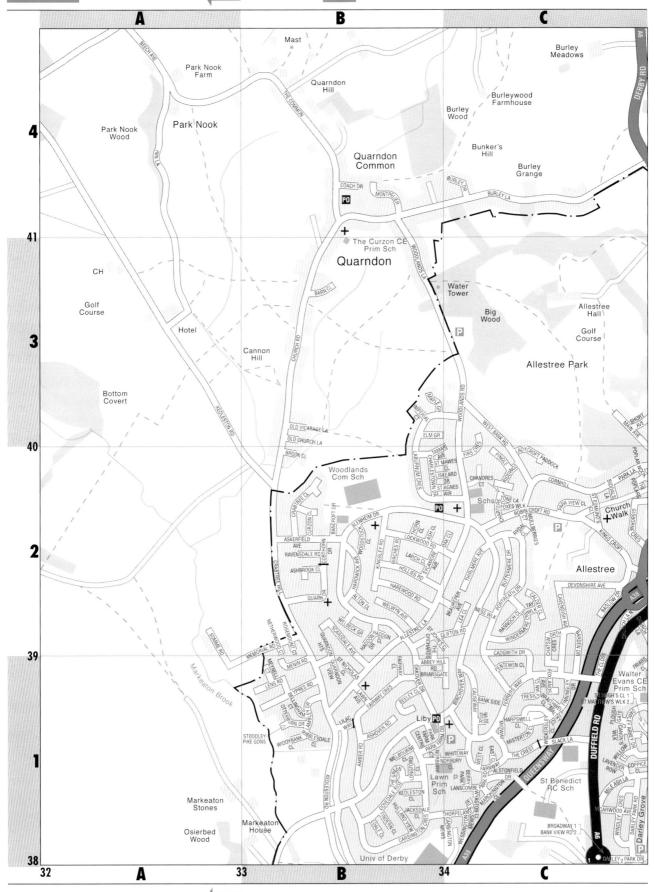

Mast

Burley
Meadows

Park Nook
Farm

BEECH AVE

Quarndon
Hill

Burleywood
Farmhouse

DERBY RD

A6

Park Nook
Wood

Park Nook

INN LA

Burley
Wood

Bunker's
Hill

4

Burley
Grange

CH

Quarndon
Common

BURLEY DR

THE COMMON

BURLEY LA

Golf
Course

COACH DR

PO

MONTPELIER

41

The Curzon CE
Prim Sch

Quarndon

WOODLANDS LA

Water
Tower

Allestree
Hall

Golf
Course

Hotel

BARN CL

CHURCH RD

KEDLESTON RD

3

Big
Wood

Allestree Park

Cannon
Hill

P

Bottom
Covert

MAPLE GR
IMPERIAL

SHORT
MAIN AVE

WEST BANK RD

POPLAR NOOK

PARK LA

POPLAR DR

OLD VICARAGE LA

ELM GR

40

OLD CHURCH LA

FIRS CRES

PINGLE
LADYCROFT PADDOCK

BROOK CL

TAMAR
AVE
ST MAWES
CL
LISKEARD
DR
ST AGNES
AVE

CHARLESTON

LABURNUM CRES

CHANDRES
CT

CORNHILL

ST EDMONDS CL

PARK VIEW CL

Woodlands
Com Sch

CRABTREE CL

BANCROFT DR

BLENHEIM DR

WOODSTOCK DR

KINGSLEY RD

BIRCHES RD

ASH CL

LOCKWOOD RD

DAY CL

PO

Schs

TONE LA
FOXES WLK

ROBIN CROFT RD

RYDAL

NILL BERRIES

P

Church
Walk

KINGS CROFT

GOSFORTH CRES

ASKERFIELD
AVE
RAVENSDALE RD

CURZON CL

THORN

LARCH CL
CLANGRE
AVE

CHAFFERS

P

CRABTREE HILL

ASHBROOK CL

HARDWICK AVE

HOLLIES RD

THIRLMERE AVE

BUTTERMERE DR

2

QUARN DR

HAREWOOD RD

WELWYN AVE

ALTON CL

Allestree

DEVONSHIRE AVE

ROSSMOUNT CT

NETHERWOOD CT

SCARSDALE AVE

WELBECK GR

HADDON

ALLESTREE LA

CLIFTON RD

BEAUFER

LEA CL

RAINBOLT CL

CAUTER CL
TAYLOR

CAVENDISH AVE

SOMME RD

MEMORIAL RD

MENELL CT

QUARNDON VIEW

HADDON

ST JOHN'S CL

The ORCHARDS

PORTREATH DR

WINDERMERE AVE

GARDEN DR
BASLOW DR

A38

39

MENIN RD

ST NICHOLAS
CL

ABBEY HILL
RD
BRIARSGATE

CADGWITH DR

PENTEWEN CL

CHATSWORTH
CRES

The CLOSE

Walter
Evans CE
Prim Sch

FRIARS

Markeaton Brook

LENS RD

BELLINGHAM

YPRES RD

OTTERBURN DR

LAMBLEY DR

FAIRWAY

BEELEY CL

LAWN
AVE

FAIRWAY CRES

BIRCHOVER WAY

OAKOVER DR

CAUSEWAY

BANK SIDE

FERRERS WAY

THE RISE

BRAITHWELL CL

TRESLA

TWINING

SLOUGH'S CL 1
ST MATTHEW'S WLK 2

STAPLEHURST

STOODLEY
PIKE GDNS

WIDDYBANK
CL

RIBBLESDALE
CL

LILAC
WAY

ASHOVER RD

AMBER RD

LANSCOMBE

WHITEWAY

WEST CL

FAIRWAY

HARPSWELL
CL

MISTERTON

THE CREST

WICKERSLEY

SLACK LA

LAVENDER
ROW

COPPICE

1

MELBOURNE
CL

LONGFORD

KEDLESTON
CL

DOVEDALE
THE GREEN

PARK
CENTRE

NORBURY
CL

Liby PO

P

Lawn
Prim
Sch

ALSTONFIELD
DR

QUEENSWAY

St Benedict
RC Sch

MILE ASH LA

VICARWOOD AVE

DARLEY PARK RD

A6

Markeaton
Stones

HULLAND VIEW

JACKSDALE
CL

FINDERN CL

EDALE CL

CARSING CL

THORPELANDS

WESSINGTON
MEWS

NORMANTON

BROADWAY 1
BANK VIEW RD 2

WINDLEY
CRES

DARLEY PARK DR

Osierbed
Wood

Markeaton
House

DUFFIELD RD

P

Univ of Derby

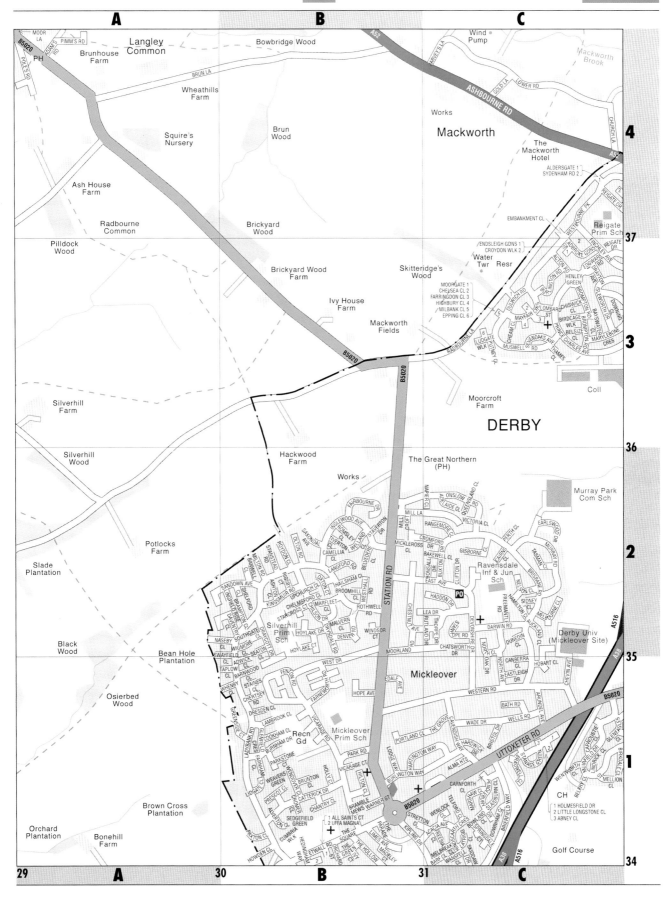

How to use the index

Street names are listed alphabetically and show the locality, the Postcode District, the page number and a reference to the square in which the name falls on the map page

Albert St. Ripley DE5 .... 10 C1

Full street name
This may have been abbreviated on the map

Town, village or locality
in which the street falls. This may be indicated by one of the abbreviations listed below

Postcode District
for the street name

Page number
of the map on which the street name appears

Grid square
in which the centre of the street falls

Schools, hospitals, sports centres, railway stations, shopping centres, industrial estates, public amenities and other places of interest are also listed.

Abbreviations used in the index

App	Approach	Ctr	Centre	Dr	Drive	Hts	Heights	Pas	Passage	Strs	Stairs
Arc	Arcade	Cir	Circus	Dro	Drove	Ind Est	Industrial Estate	Pl	Place	Stps	Steps
Ave	Avenue	Cl	Close	E	East	Intc	Interchange	Prec	Precinct	St	Street, Saint
Bvd	Boulevard	Comm	Common	Emb	Embankment	Junc	Junction	Prom	Promenade	Terr	Terrace
Bldgs	Buildings	Cnr	Corner	Espl	Esplanade	La	Lane	Ret Pk	Retail Park	Trad Est	Trading Estate
Bsns Pk	Business Park	Cotts	Cottages	Est	Estate	N	North	Rd	Road	Wlk	Walk
Bsns Ctr	Business Centre	Ct	Court	Gdns	Gardens	Orch	Orchard	Rdbt	Roundabout	W	West
Bglws	Bungalows	Ctyd	Courtyard	Gn	Green	Par	Parade	S	South	Yd	Yard
Cswy	Causeway	Cres	Crescent	Gr	Grove	Pk	Park	Sq	Square		

Abbreviations of town, village and rural locality names

Aldercar	Ald	Dethick	Det	Horsley Woodhouse		Mackworth	Mack	Shottle	Shot
Alderwasley	Alder	Derby	Derby		H Wood	Mapperley	Mapp	Smalley	Smal
Alfreton	Alf	Duffield	Duff	Idridgehay	Idri	Nether Heage	N Heage	Somercotes	Som
Alton	Alton	Eastwood	East	Ilkeston	Ilk	Pentrich	Pent	South Wingfield	S Wing
Ambergate	Amber	Fritchley	Fritch	Ironville	Iron	Postern	Post	Spout	Spout
Ashleyhay	Ash	Hazelwood	Haz	Kedleston	Kedl	Quarndon	Quar	Swanwick	Swan
Belper	Belper	Heage	Heage	Kilburn	Kilb	Ravendale Park	Raven Pk	Toadmoor	Toad
Bullbridge	Bullbr	Heanor	Hean	Kirk Langley	K Lang	Riddings	Ridd	Turnditch	Turn
Codnor	Codnor	Holbrook	Holbr	Langley Mill	La Mill	Ridgeway	Ridge	Weston Underwood	
Crich	Crich	Holloway	Hollow	Lea	Lea	Ripley	Ripley		W Und
Denby	Denby	Horsley	Hors	Loscoe	Los	Shipley	Ship	Windley	Wind

Abbey Hill Rd. Derby DE22 .... 28 B1	**Aldersgate.** Derby DE22 .... 29 C4	**Amber Ct.** Hean DE75 .... 17 C1	**Ash St.** Ilk DE7 .... 25 C2
Abbey St. Ilk DE7 .... 25 C1	**Aldred's La.** Hean DE75, NG1618 A1	**Amber Dr.** Hean NG16 .... 18 A1	**Ash Tree Cl.** Duff DE56 .... 21 C3
Abbots Gr. Belper DE56 .... 15 A3	**Alexander St.** East NG16 .... 18 C1	**Amber Gr.** Alf DE55 .... 4 C1	**Ashbourne Rd.** Belper DE56 ... 14 B2
Abbotsford Mews. Ilk DE7 ...... 25 B2	**Alfred Rd.** Kilb DE56 .... 23 A4	**Amber Hill.** Crich DE4 .... 9 A4	**Ashbourne Rd.** K Lang DE6 ... 26 B2
Abbott Rd. Alf DE55 .... 5 A2	**Alfred St.** Alf DE55 .... 4 C2	**Amber Hts.** Ripley DE5 .... 10 B1	**Ashbourne Rd.** Mack DE22 .... 29 C4
Abbott St. Hean DE75 .... 17 C1	**Alfred St.** Ripley DE5 .... 10 C1	**Amber Rd.** Bullbr DE56 .... 9 A3	**Ashbourne Rd.** Shot DE56 .... 13 B2
Abells. Denby DE5 .... 16 B1	**Alfred St.** Som DE55 .... 11 B3	**Amber Rd.** Derby DE22 .... 28 B1	**Ashbourne Rd.** Turn DE56 ..... 13 B2
Abney Cl. Derby DE3 .... 29 C1	**Alfred St.** S Norm DE55 .... 5 C3	**Amber View Rd.** Fritch DE56 ... 9 A4	**Ashbrook Cl.** Derby DE22 ...... 28 B2
Acacia Ave. Derby DE3 .... 29 C1	**Alfreton L Ctr.** Alf DE55 .... 4 C2	**Ambergate Prim Sch.** Amber	**Asher La.** Pent DE5 .... 10 B3
Acorn Dr. Belper DE56 .... 15 A3	**Alfreton Sta.** Alf DE55 .... 5 B3	DE56 .... 8 C2	**Ashfield Ave.** Som DE55 .... 5 B1
Acorn Way. Belper DE56 .... 15 A3	**Alfreton Rd.** Codnor DE5 .... 11 B1	**Ambergate Sta.** Amber DE56 .. 8 C2	**Ashford Pl.** Ilk DE7 .... 25 C3
Acton Rd. Derby DE22 .... 29 C3	**Alfreton Rd.** Holbr DE21 .... 22 B3	**Ambergrove.** Ridge DE56 .... 9 A3	**Ashford Rise.** Belper DE56 .... 15 B3
Adale Rd. Smal DE7 .... 24 A4	**Alfreton Trad Est.** Alf DE55 .... 5 A1	**Ambleside Dr.** East NG16 ...... 18 B2	**Ashforth Ave.** Hean DE75 ...... 18 A1
Adam Bede Cres. Wirk DE4 .... 6 C3	**All Saints Ct.** Derby DE3 .... 29 B1	**American Adventure Theme Pk.**	**Ashley Cl.** Tans DE4 .... 1 A2
Adam's Rd. K Lang DE6 .... 29 A4	**Allan La.** Fritch DE56 .... 9 A3	Ship DE75 .... 25 A3	**Ashop Rd.** Belper DE56 .... 15 B3
Adams Cl. Ship DE75 .... 24 B4	**Allandale Rd.** Hean DE75 ...... 17 B1	**Anchor Rd.** East NG16 .... 18 B1	**Ashover Rd.** Derby DE22 .... 28 B1
Adams Ct. Ilk DE7 .... 25 C2	**Allen La.** Ash DE4 .... 1 B3	**Andrews Dr.** La Mill NG16 ..... 18 A2	**Ashton Cl.** Derby DE3 .... 29 B2
Addison Dr. Alf DE55 .... 5 A2	**Allen La.** W Und DE6 .... 19 B1	**Andrews Dr.** Stanl DE7 .... 24 A1	**Ashton Cl.** Swan DE55 .... 11 A4
Addison Villas. East NG16 ..... 18 C1	**Allestree La.** Derby DE22 ...... 28 B2	**Anson Wlk.** Ilk DE7 .... 25 C2	**Ashton Way.** Belper DE56 ...... 15 B2
Adelaide Cl. Derby DE3 .... 29 C2	**Allissa Ave.** Ripley DE5 .... 16 C4	**Anthony Fell Sch.** Wirk DE4 .... 6 C4	**Askerfield Ave.** Derby DE22 ... 28 B2
Adelaide Wlk. Iron NG16 .... 11 C2	**Allstone Lee.** Belper DE56 ..... 14 C3	**Appleton Dr.** Belper DE56 ...... 15 A3	**Astcote Cl.** Hean DE75 .... 18 A1
Admiral Cl. Hean DE75 .... 17 B1	**Alma Hts.** Derby DE3 .... 29 C1	**Applewood Cl.** Belper DE56 ... 15 A3	**Astlow Dr.** Belper DE56 .... 15 A3
Adwick Cl. Derby DE3 .... 29 B1	**Alma St.** Alf DE55 .... 5 A2	**Archer St.** Ilk DE7 .... 25 C2	**Aston Ct.** Ilk DE7 .... 25 C1
Albert Rd. Ripley DE5 .... 10 B1	**Alma St.** Ripley DE5 .... 10 B2	**Ardsley Cl.** Hean DE75 .... 18 A1	**Atherfield Gdns.** East NG16 ... 18 C2
Albert St. Belper DE56 .... 14 C2	**Almond Ave.** Ripley DE5 .... 16 B4	**Argyle St.** La Mill NG16 .... 18 B2	**Atherton Rd.** Ilk DE7 .... 25 B2
Albert St. East NG16 .... 18 C2	**Almond Gr.** Swan DE55 .... 11 A4	**Argyll Rd.** Ripley DE5 .... 10 C1	**Atherton Rd.** Ship DE7 .... 25 B2
Albert St. Iron NG16 .... 11 C3	**Alport Cl.** Belper DE56 .... 15 A3	**Arkwright Ave.** Belper DE56 ... 15 B3	**Auckland Cl.** Derby DE3 .... 29 C2
Albert St. Ripley DE5 .... 10 C1	**Alport La.** Spout DE56 .... 7 B2	**Arkwright St.** Wirk DE4 .... 6 C4	**Audley Cl.** Ilk DE7 .... 25 B2
Albert St. Som DE55 .... 11 A4	**Alstonfield Dr.** Derby DE22 ... 28 C1	**Arlington Dr.** Swan DE55 .... 10 C4	**Avenue Rd.** Duff DE56 .... 21 C3
Albion St. Ilk DE7 .... 25 C1	**Althorp Cl.** Swan DE55 .... 10 C4	**Arthur St.** Alf DE55 .... 5 A3	**Avenue The.** Belper DE56 ...... 14 C1
Albion St. Ripley DE5 .... 10 C1	**Alton Cl.** Derby DE22 .... 28 B2	**Arundel Ave.** Derby DE3 .... 29 C1	**Avis Ave.** Hean DE75 .... 24 C4
Alder Rd. Belper DE56 .... 15 A2	**Alton Rd.** Belper DE56 .... 15 B2	**Ash Acre.** Belper DE56 .... 15 B2	**Awsworth Rd.** Ilk DE7 .... 25 C1
Aldercar Inf Sch. Ald NG16 ... 18 A2	**Alvenor St.** Ilk DE7 .... 25 C1	**Ash Cl.** Derby DE22 .... 28 B2	**Azalea Ave.** Swan DE55 .... 11 A4
Aldercar La. Ald NG16 .... 18 A3	**Alverton Cl.** Derby DE3 .... 29 B1	**Ash Cres.** Ripley DE5 .... 16 B4	**Azalea Cl.** Alf DE55 .... 5 C2
Aldercar Sch. Ald NG16 .... 18 A2	**Amber Cl.** Bullbr DE56 .... 9 A3	**Ash Gr.** Brin NG16 .... 18 B4	
Alders La. Tans DE4 .... 1 A2	**Amber Ct.** Belper DE56 .... 15 A3	**Ash Mount Rd.** La Mill NG16 .. 18 A2	

Babington Hospl. Belper DE56 14 C1
Back La. Alder DE56 .... 7 C4
Back La. Ilk DE7 .... 25 C1
Back La. Pent DE5 .... 10 B3
Back La. Spout DE56 .... 7 B2
Back La. Wess DE55 .... 3 C4
Back Wyver La. Belper DE56 . 14 C3
Bacon La. Pent DE5 .... 10 A3
Bailey Brook Cres. La Mill ....
NG16 .... 18 A2
Bailey Brook Dr. La Mill NG16 18 A2
Bailey Brook Ind Est. Hean ....
DE75, NG16 .... 18 A1
Bailey Brook Wlk. La Mill ....
NG16 .... 18 A2
Bailey Grove Rd. East NG16 .. 18 B1
Baker Ave. Hean DE75 .... 24 C4
Baker Cl. Som DE55 .... 11 B4
Baker Cl. Stanl DE7 .... 24 A1
Baker St. Ilk DE7 .... 25 C1
Bakers Hill. Heage DE56 .... 9 C1
Bakers La. Hollow DE4 .... 2 A4
Bakewell Cl. Derby DE3 .... 29 C2
Ballacraine Dr. Ripley DE5 ... 10 C1
Balmoral Cl. Hean DE75 .... 17 B1
Bamford St. Ripley DE5 .... 16 B4
Bancroft Dr. Derby DE22 .... 28 B2
Bank Side. Derby DE22 .... 28 C1
Bank St. La Mill NG16 .... 18 B2
Bank St. Som DE55 .... 11 B4
Bank View Rd. N Heage DE56 .. 9 B1
Banksburn Cl. Hean DE75 .... 17 B1
Banwell Cl. Derby DE3 .... 29 B2
Barber Cl. Ilk DE7 .... 25 C2
Barclay Ct. Ship DE7 .... 25 B2
Barden Dr. Derby DE22 .... 28 C2
Barf Cl. Derby DE3 .... 29 C1
Bargate Cl. Belper DE56 .... 15 A1
Bargate Rd. Belper DE56 .... 15 A1
Barker Gate. Ilk DE7 .... 25 C1
Barley Croft. Belper DE56 ...... 15 A1
Barling Dr. Ilk DE7 .... 25 B1
Barling Dr. Ship DE7 .... 25 B1
Barn Cl. Quar DE22 .... 28 B3
Barnsley La. Idri DE56 .... 6 C1
Barnsley La. Spout DE56 .... 6 C1
Barnwood Cl. Derby DE3 .... 29 B1
Barrack Yd. Som DE55 .... 11 B4
Barton Knoll. Belper DE56 ...... 15 B2
Barton Knowle. Belper DE56 .. 15 B2
Baslow Dr. Derby DE22 .... 28 C2
Bassford Ave. Hean DE75 ...... 17 C1
Bath Rd. Derby DE3 .... 29 C1
Bath St. Ilk DE7 .... 25 C1
Bayswater Cl. Derby DE22 ..... 29 C3
Beatty Wlk. Ilk DE7 .... 25 C2
Beauchief Gdns. Som DE55 ... 11 B4
Beaulieu Way. Swan DE55 ..... 11 A4
Beaumont Cl. Belper DE56 ..... 15 B2
Beaurepaire Cres. Belper DE56 ......
.... 15 A3
Beaureper Ave. Derby DE22 .. 28 C2
Beauvale Dr. Ilk DE7 .... 25 C3
Becksitch La. Belper DE56 ..... 14 C1
Beech Ave. Alf DE55 .... 5 A3
Beech Ave. Quar DE22 .... 28 A4
Beech Ave. Ripley DE5 .... 10 B1
Beech Cl. Belper DE56 .... 15 A2
Beech Cl. Kilb DE56 .... 23 A4
Beechdale Rd. Alf DE55 .... 5 B2
Beeches The. Crich DE4 .... 2 C1
Beeches The. Hean DE75 ...... 24 B4
Beechwood Cl. Belper DE56 .. 14 C3
Beeley Cl. Belper DE56 .... 15 B3
Beeley Cl. Derby DE22 .... 28 B2
Beighton St. Ripley DE5 ...... 10 C1
Belfield Ct. Hean DE75 .... 17 B2
Belfry Cl. Derby DE3 .... 29 C1
Belgrave Cl. Belper DE56 ...... 15 B3
Bell La. Smal DE7 .... 23 C2
Belle Acre Cl. Belper DE56 ... 14 C2
Belle Vue Ave. Ripley DE5 ... 16 B3
Belledere Cl. Swan DE55 ...... 10 C4
Bellingham Ct. Derby DE22 ... 28 B1

Belper La. Belper DE56 .... 14 C3
Belper Rd. Holbr DE56 .... 22 B4
Belper Rd. Kilb DE56 .... 15 C1
Belper Rd. Morley DE7 .... 23 C1
Belper Rd. Stanl DE7 .... 24 A1
Belper Sch. Belper DE56 ...... 15 B2
Belper Sports Ctr. Belper DE5615 B2
Belper Sta. Belper DE56 ...... 14 C2
Belsize Cl. Derby DE22 .... 29 C3
Belton Dr. Ripley DE5 .... 10 C1
Belvedere Cl. Derby DE3 ...... 29 B2
Belvoir Way. Som DE55 .... 5 B1
Benjamin Outram Bsns Ctr. ....
Ripley DE5 .... 16 C4
Bennerley Ave. Ilk DE7 .... 25 C2
Bennerley Fields Sch. Ilk DE7 25 C2
Bennerley Sch. Ilk DE7 .... 25 C2
Bennetts La. Crich DE4 .... 9 A4
Bent La. Spout DE56 .... 7 B3
Bent La. Wirk DE56 .... 7 B3
Bentfield Rd. N Heage DE56 ... 9 B1
Bentley Cl. Alf DE55 .... 5 A2
Beresford Dr. Ilk DE7 .... 25 C3
Beresford Pl. Bullbr DE56 ..... 9 A3
Berle Ave. Hean DE75 .... 17 C1
Berry Park Cl. Derby DE22 .... 28 C1
Bessalone Dr. Belper DE56 ... 15 A3
Bestwick Ave. Hean DE75 ..... 18 A1
Bideford Cl. Ripley DE5 ...... 10 B1
Biggin La. H Ward DE6 .... 12 A2
Bigginmill La. K Ire DE56 ..... 12 B3
Birch Ave. Toad DE56 .... 8 C2
Birch Cl. Alf DE55 .... 5 A3
Birch Cl. Ripley DE5 .... 16 B4
Birch Cl. Wess DE55 .... 3 C4
Birches Ave. S Wing DE55 ..... 3 C3
Birches La. S Wing DE55 ...... 4 A3
Birches Rd. Ridge DE56 .... 28 B2
Birchfield Pk. Hean DE75 ..... 24 C4
Birchover Pl. Ilk DE7 .... 25 C3
Birchover Way. Derby DE22 .. 28 C1
Birchview Cl. Belper DE56 .... 15 A1
Birchwood. Hean DE75 .... 17 B2
Birchwood Cres. Som DE55 ... 11 B4
Birchwood Dr. Ridge DE56 ..... 9 A2
Birchwood La. Pinx DE55 ...... 5 C2
Birchwood La. Som DE55 ...... 5 C2
Birchwood La. S Norm DE55 ... 5 C2
Birchwood Rd. Alf DE55 .... 5 B2
Birchwood Way. Som DE55 ..... 5 B1
Bircumshaw's Rd. Hean DE75 17 C1
Birdcage Wlk. Derby DE22 .... 29 C3
Birkdale Cl. Ilk DE7 .... 25 B1
Bishop St. Alf DE55 .... 5 A3
Bishop St. East NG16 .... 18 C1
Blackberry Way. Kilb DE56 ... 15 C1
Blackbird Row. Holbr DE56 .... 15 B1
Blackburn Pl. Ilk DE7 .... 25 C2
Blackden Cl. Belper DE56 ...... 15 C2
Blackstone Cl. Som DE55 ...... 11 B4
Blackthorne Cl. Kilb DE56 ..... 15 C1
Blackwall La. K Ire DE56 ...... 12 A4
Blake St. Ilk DE7 .... 25 C1
Blenheim Ave. Swan DE55 ..... 11 A4
Blenheim Ct. Belper DE56 ..... 15 B3
Blenheim Dr. Derby DE22 ..... 28 B2
Blind La. K Ire DE6 .... 6 A1
Blind La. Wirk DE4 .... 6 C4
Blissworth Way. Swan DE55 .. 10 C4
Bloomfield Rd. Swan DE55 .... 11 A4
Bloomgrove Rd. Ilk DE7 .... 25 C1
Bluebell Cl. Som DE55 .... 5 C1
Blundestone La. Wirk DE4 ..... 2 A1
Blunt St. Stanl DE7 .... 24 A1
Boat La. Ald NG16 .... 18 A4
Boatmans Cl. Ilk DE7 .... 25 C1
Bobbinmill Hill. Fritch DE56 ... 9 A4
Bolsover Cl. Ripley DE5 ...... 10 C1
Bolton St. Swan DE55 .... 10 B4
Bond La. Heage DE56 .... 9 C1
Bonnington Dr. Som DE55 .... 11 B4
Bonsall Dr. Derby DE3 .... 29 C2
Bonsall La. Alf DE55 .... 4 C2
Bonsalt Dr. Som DE55 .... 11 B4

Booth St. Ripley DE5 .... 10 C1
Boothgate. Heage DE56 .... 15 C4
Boscowan Ct. Ilk DE7 .... 25 C2
Bosley Mews. Belper DE56 ... 14 C3
Botany Dr. Ilk DE7 .... 25 C3
Bottom Lons. K Ire DE56 ..... 12 A4
Boughton Dr. Swan DE55 ...... 10 C4
Boundary La. East NG16 ...... 18 B2
Bournebrook Ave. Wirk DE4 .... 6 C4
Bowes Well Rd. Ilk DE7 .... 25 C1
Bowland Cl. Derby DE3 .... 29 C1
Bowler Dr. Kilb DE56 .... 23 A4
Bowler St. Ripley DE5 .... 16 B4
Bowling Alley. Heage DE56 ..... 9 C1
Bowman's La. Shot DE56 ...... 13 C4
Bowmer La. Fritch DE56 .... 9 A3
Bown Cl. Kilb DE56 .... 23 A4
Bowns Hill. Crich DE4 .... 3 A1
Bracken La. Hollow DE4 .... 2 A3
Brackendale Rd. Swan DE55 . 10 C4
Brackenfield La. Wess DE55 ... 3 B4
Brackley. Kilb DE56 .... 15 C1
Brackley Gate. Morley DE7 .... 23 A1
Bradgate Dr. Ripley DE5 ...... 10 A1
Bradley Dr. Belper DE56 ...... 15 A2
Bradshaw Ave. Som DE55 ..... 11 C3
Bradshaw Croft. Belper DE56 14 C3
Bradshaw Dr. Holbr DE56 ..... 22 B3
Bradwell Cl. Derby DE3 .... 29 C1
Bradwell Way. Belper DE56 ... 15 A3
Braemar Ave. East NG16 ...... 18 C1
Brafield Cl. Belper DE56 ...... 15 B2
Braithwell Ct. Derby DE22 .... 28 C1
Bramble Mews. Derby DE3 .... 29 B1
Bramble Way. Kilb DE56 ...... 15 C1
Bramley St. Som DE55 .... 11 C4
Brampton Ave. Hean DE75 .... 18 A1
Brampton Cl. Derby DE3 .... 29 B2
Brampton Ct. Belper DE56 .... 15 B2
Braybrook Cl. Swan DE55 ..... 10 C4
Breach Rd. Denby DE5 .... 17 A2
Breach Rd. Hean DE75 .... 25 A4
Breadsall Cl. Ilk DE7 .... 25 C2
Breamfield La. Wirk DE56 ..... 7 A4
Brenden Ave. Som DE55 .... 11 B4
Brenden Cl. Som DE55 .... 11 B4
Bretton Rd. Belper DE56 ...... 15 C3
Briar Cl. Alf DE55 .... 5 B2
Briar's La. Crich DE4 .... 9 A4
Briars Way. Ripley DE5 .... 16 B4
Briarsgate. Derby DE22 .... 28 B1
Brickyard La. Kilb DE56 ...... 15 C1
Brickyard La. Ripley DE5 ...... 10 C1
Brickyard Rd. Bullbr DE56 ..... 9 B3
Brickyard The. Stanl DE7 ..... 24 A1
Bridge Foot. Belper DE56 ..... 14 C3
Bridge Hill. Belper DE56 ...... 14 C3
Bridge St. Belper DE56 .... 14 C2
Bridge St. Ilk DE7 .... 25 C2
Bridge St. La Mill NG16 .... 18 B2
Bridge View. Belper DE56 ..... 22 A4
Bridle La. Ripley DE5 .... 10 C1
Bridle La. Ripley DE5 .... 10 A1
Bridle La. Som DE55 .... 11 A4
Bright St. Ilk DE7 .... 25 C2
Bright St. S Norm DE55 .... 5 C3
Brinsley Prim Sch. Brin NG16 18 B4
Brisbane Rd. Derby DE3 .... 29 C2
Bristol Dr. Derby DE3 .... 29 C1
Bristol Rd. Ilk DE7 .... 25 C1
Britannia Ave. Ripley DE5 ..... 17 A4
Brittain Dr. Ripley DE5 .... 11 A1
Broad La. Brin NG16 .... 18 C4
Broad Oak Dr. Brin NG16 ..... 18 C4
Broad Way. K Ire DE56 .... 12 A4
Broadholme La. Belper DE56 . 15 A4
Broadway. Duff DE56 .... 21 C1
Broadway. Hean DE75 .... 17 C1
Broadway. Ilk DE7 .... 25 C2
Broadway. Ripley DE5 .... 10 C1
Broadway. Swan DE55 .... 10 C4
Broadway Ave. Ripley DE5 .... 10 C1
Broadway Ct. Ripley DE5 ...... 10 C1
Brockhall Rise. Hean DE75 ... 18 A1

Brompton Rd. Derby DE22 .... 29 C3
Brook Ave. Alf DE55 .... 5 A2
Brook Cl. Alf DE55 .... 5 A2
Brook Cl. Quar DE22 .... 28 B2
Brook Cotts. Ilk DE7 .... 25 C2
Brook Ct. Hean NG16 .... 18 A1
Brook La. Alf DE55 .... 5 A2
Brook La. Crich DE56 .... 9 B3
Brook La. Ripley DE5 .... 16 B4
Brook St. Heage DE56 .... 9 C1
Brook St. Hean DE75 .... 17 A3
Brook St. N Heage DE56 .... 9 B1
Brook Vale Rd. La Mill NG16 . 18 B1
Brookfield Cl. Codnor DE5 .... 11 A1
Brookfield Way. Hean DE75 ... 18 A1
Brookfields. Hors DE56 .... 22 C4
Brookhill Leys Rd. East NG16 18 C1
Brooklands Ave. Hean DE75 .. 17 C1
Brooklands Ave. Wirk DE4 .... 6 C4
Brookside. Belper DE56 .... 14 C2
Brookside. East NG16 .... 18 C2
Brookvale Ave. Codnor DE5 ... 17 A4
Brookvale Ave. Denby DE5 .... 16 A1
Brookvale Rd. Denby DE5 ..... 16 A1
Brookvale Rise. Denby DE5 ... 16 A1
Broom Ave. Swan DE55 .... 10 C4
Broom Cl. Belper DE56 .... 14 C3
Broom Cl. Duff DE56 .... 21 B2
Broomhill Cl. Derby DE3 ..... 29 B2
Broughton Cl. Ilk DE7 .... 25 B1
Brown's La. Holbr DE56 ...... 22 B4
Brown's Yd. Som DE55 .... 11 B4
Brun La. K Lang DE6 .... 29 A4
Brun La. Mack DE22 .... 29 A4
Brunton Cl. Derby DE3 .... 29 B1
Brussels Terr. Ilk DE7 .... 25 C1
Brynsmoor Rd. Brin NG16 .... 18 C4
Buckfast Cl. Swan DE55 ...... 10 C4
Buckhazels La. Mack DE6 ..... 27 A4
Buckingham Cl. Swan DE55 .. 11 A4
Bullbridge Hill. Bullbr DE56 ... 9 A3
Bullhill La. H Ward DE56 ...... 12 C2
Bullhurst La. W Und DE6 ...... 19 C2
Bulling La. Crich DE4 .... 2 C1
Bullock La. Iron NG16 .... 11 C3
Bullock La. Som DE55 .... 11 C3
Bullsmoor. Belper DE56 .... 15 B2
Burbage Cl. Belper DE56 ...... 15 B3
Burke Dr. Som DE55 .... 11 B4
Burland Green La. W Und DE6 ....
.... 20 A2
Burleigh Cres. Swan DE55 .... 10 C4
Burleigh St. Ilk DE7 .... 25 C1
Burley Dr. Quar DE22 .... 28 C4
Burley La. Quar DE22 .... 28 C4
Burlington Rd. Derby DE22 ... 29 C3
Burlington Way. Derby DE3 ... 29 B1
Burnham Dr. Derby DE3 .... 29 B1
Burns St. Hean DE75 .... 17 B1
Burnt House Rd. Hean DE75 .. 17 B1
Burr La. Ilk DE7 .... 25 C1
Burton St. Hean DE75 .... 17 C1
Bush Vale. Belper DE56 .... 14 C3
Butterfield Cres. Swan DE55 . 10 C4
Butterley Croft Bsns Ctr. ....
Ripley DE5 .... 16 C4
Butterley Hill. Ripley DE5 .... 10 C2
Butterley La. Ash S45 .... 1 C3
Butterley La. Ripley DE5 ...... 10 B2
Buttermere Dr. Derby DE22 .. 28 C2
Butts The. Belper DE56 .... 15 A2
Buxton Ave. Hean DE75 .... 24 C4
Buxton Ct. Ilk DE7 .... 25 B1
Buxton Dr. Derby DE3 .... 29 C2
Buxton Dr. Lit Ea DE21 .... 22 B1
Byron Ave. Alf DE55 .... 5 A2
Byron St. Ilk DE7 .... 25 C1
Bywell La. Kilb DE56 .... 15 C1

Cadeby Ct. Som DE55 .... 11 B3
Cadgwith Dr. Derby DE22 .... 28 C2
Caernarfon Cl. Swan DE55 ... 11 A4
Cairns Cl. Derby DE3 .... 29 C2

Calder Cl. Derby DE22 .... 28 C2
Calke Rise. Ripley DE5 .... 10 C1
Calladine La. H Wood DE7 .... 23 B3
Calladine La. Shot DE56 .... 13 B3
Calladine Rd. Hean DE75 ...... 17 B1
Callow La. Callow DE4 .... 6 B3
Callow La. Wirk DE4 .... 6 B3
Calver Cl. Belper DE56 .... 15 A3
Camellia Cl. Derby DE3 .... 29 B2
Campbell St. Belper DE56 ...... 14 C2
Campbell St. La Mill NG16 ...... 18 B2
Canada St. Belper DE56 .... 15 A1
Canberra Cl. Derby DE3 .... 29 C1
Canon Cl. Ilk DE7 .... 25 C3
Canon's Wlk. Derby DE22 ...... 28 C1
Canterbury Cl. Duff DE56 .... 21 C2
Canterbury Rd. Wirk DE4 .... 6 C4
Canterbury Terr. Wirk DE4 .... 6 C4
Cantley Rd. Som DE55 .... 11 B3
Carlton Cl. Hean DE75 .... 18 A2
Carlyle Pl. Hean DE75 .... 17 B2
Carlyle St. Hean DE75 .... 17 B2
Carnfield Hall. S Norm DE55 ... 5 B3
Carnfield Hill. S Norm DE55 .... 5 B3
Carnforth Cl. Derby DE3 .... 29 C1
Carnoustie Cl. Derby DE3 ...... 29 C1
Carr Fields. H Wood DE7 .... 23 B4
Carr La. Crich DE4 .... 2 C1
Carrock Ave. Hean DE75 .... 18 A1
Carsington Cres. Derby DE22 .. 28 B1
Carsington Mews. Derby DE22 28 C1
Casson St. Iron NG16 .... 11 C2
Castle Dr. Codnor NG16 .... 17 C4
Castle Dr. Som DE55 .... 11 B4
Castle Hill. Duff DE56 .... 21 C2
Castle La. Iron NG16 .... 11 C1
Castle Orch. Duff DE56 .... 21 C2
Castle View. Ald NG16 .... 18 A2
Castlefields. Iron NG16 .... 11 C2
Castleton Ave. Ilk DE7 .... 25 C3
Castleton Ave. Som DE55 ...... 11 B3
Catherine St. Alf DE55 .... 5 B2
Catterick Dr. Derby DE3 .... 29 B1
Causeway. Derby DE22 .... 28 C1
Causeway The. Wirk DE4 .... 6 C4
Cavendish Ave. Derby DE22 .. 28 C2
Cavendish Cl. Duff DE56 .... 21 B1
Cavendish Dr. Ripley DE5 ...... 10 B1
Cavendish Way. Derby DE3 ... 29 C1
Cedar Ave. Alf DE55 .... 5 A3
Cedar Ave. Ripley DE5 .... 10 B1
Cedar Croft. Kilb DE56 .... 23 A4
Cedar Gr. Belper DE56 .... 15 A1
Cemetery La. Ripley DE5 .... 10 C1
Cemetery Rd. Belper DE56 .... 15 A3
Cemetery Rd. Som DE55 .... 11 B4
Central Rd. Alf DE55 .... 5 A2
Chadfield Rd. Duff DE56 .... 21 C3
Chadwick Nick La. Crich DE4 ... 8 C4
Chalons Cl. Ilk DE7 .... 25 C1
Champion Ave. Ilk DE7 .... 25 B2
Champion Hill. Duff DE56 ...... 21 C2
Chandres Ct. Derby DE22 ..... 28 C2
Chantry Cl. Derby DE73 .... 29 B1
Chapel Ct. Ilk DE7 .... 25 C2
Chapel La. Crich DE4 .... 9 A4
Chapel La. Hollow DE4 .... 2 A3
Chapel Row. Crich DE4 .... 9 A4
Chapel St. Alf DE55 .... 5 A2
Chapel St. Belper DE56 .... 14 C2
Chapel St. Duff DE56 .... 21 C2
Chapel St. East NG16 .... 18 C1
Chapel St. Fritch DE56 .... 9 A3
Chapel St. Hean DE75 .... 25 A4
Chapel St. Holbr DE56 .... 22 B4
Chapel St. Kilb DE56 .... 23 A4
Chapel St. Ripley DE5 .... 10 B1
Chapel St. Som DE55 .... 11 B4
Chapel St. Swan DE55 .... 10 C4
Chapel St. Ilk DE7 .... 25 C2
Charity Rd. Som DE55 .... 11 B3
Charles St. Alf DE55 .... 5 A3
Charles St. Som DE55 .... 11 B4
Charlestown Dr. Derby DE22 . 28 B2

Charlotte Inf Sch. Ilk DE7 .... 25 C1
Charnwood Ave. Belper DE56 15 A2
Charnwood Cl. Swan DE55 .... 10 C4
Charnwood Dr. Ripley DE5 ..... 10 B1
Charterstone La. Derby DE22 28 C2
Chase Rd. Amber DE56 .... 8 C2
Chase The. Kilb DE56 .... 23 A4
Chase The. Lit Ea DE21 .... 22 B1
Chase View. Crich DE4 .... 2 C1
Chatham Ave. Alf DE55 .... 5 B2
Chatham Ct. Belper DE56 ...... 15 B2
Chatsworth Ave. Crich DE4 .... 2 C1
Chatsworth Cl. Alf DE55 .... 4 C2
Chatsworth Cres. Bullbr DE56 .. 9 A3
Chatsworth Cres. Derby DE22 28 C2
Chatsworth Dr. Derby DE3 ..... 29 C2
Chatsworth Cres. Lit Ea DE21 .. 22 B1
Chaucer Jun Sch. Ilk DE7 ..... 25 C1
Chaucer St. Ilk DE7 .... 25 C1
Cheam Cl. Derby DE22 .... 29 C3
Cheapside. Belper DE56 .... 14 C2
Chelmsford Cl. Derby DE3 ..... 29 B2
Chelsea Cl. Derby DE22 .... 29 C3
Chequer La. Shot DE56 .... 7 B1
Cheriton Dr. Ship DE7 .... 25 B2
Cherry Tree Ave. Belper DE56 15 A3
Cherry Tree Ave. Ripley DE5 .. 16 B4
Cherry Tree Cl. Brin NG16 ..... 18 C4
Cherrytree Ave. Swan DE55 ... 11 A4
Chertsey Rd. Derby DE3 .... 29 B1
Chesterfield Rd. Alf DE55 .... 4 C3
Chesterfield Rd. Alf DE55 .... 4 C3
Chesterfield Rd. Belper DE56 15 A2
Chesterfield Rd. Heage DE56 .. 9 C2
Chestnut Ave. Belper DE56 ... 15 A1
Chestnut Ave. Derby DE73 .... 29 B2
Chestnut Ave. Holbr DE56 ..... 22 B4
Chestnut Ave. Ripley DE5 ...... 16 B4
Chestnut Ave. Som DE55 ...... 11 B3
Chestnut Bank. Hean DE75 .... 17 B1
Chestnut Cl. Duff DE56 .... 21 C1
Chestnut Cl. H Wood DE7 ...... 23 B4
Chestnut Rd. La Mill NG16 .... 18 A2
Chestnut Way. Swan DE55 .... 11 A4
Chevin Ave. Derby DE72 .... 29 C1
Chevin Bank. Duff DE56 .... 21 B3
Chevin Rd. Belper DE56 .... 14 C1
Chevin Rd. Belper DE56 .... 21 C4
Chevin Rd. Duff DE56 .... 21 C3
Chevin Vale. Duff DE56 .... 21 C3
Chevin View. Belper DE56 ..... 14 C2
Cheviot Ave. Iron NG16 .... 11 C2
Chewton St. East NG16 .... 18 C1
Chilson Dr. Derby DE3 .... 29 B2
Chiswick Cl. Derby DE22 .... 29 C3
Christ the King RC Prim Sch. ....
Alf DE55 .... 5 A3
Chrysalis Way. East NG16 .... 18 B2
Church Cnr. K Ire DE6 .... 6 A1
Church Croft. Ripley DE5 .... 10 B1
Church Dr. Ilk DE7 .... 25 B2
Church La. Belper DE56 .... 15 A2
Church La. Brin NG16 .... 18 C4
Church La. Fritch DE56 .... 9 A3
Church La. H Wood DE7 .... 23 C3
Church La. K Lang DE6 .... 26 C1
Church La. Mack DE22 .... 29 C4
Church La. S Wing DE55 .... 3 C2
Church La. U Wind DE6 .... 19 C1
Church La N. Derby DE22 ...... 28 C2
Church Level. K Ire DE6 .... 6 A1
Church Rd. Quar DE22 .... 28 B3
Church Sq. Hean DE75 .... 17 C1
Church St. Alf DE55 .... 4 C2
Church St. Belper DE56 .... 15 A2
Church St. Denby DE5 .... 16 B1
Church St. East NG16 .... 18 C1
Church St. Fritch DE56 .... 9 A3
Church St. Heage DE56 .... 9 C2
Church St. Hean DE75 .... 17 C1
Church St. Holbr DE56 .... 22 B3
Church St. Hollow DE4 .... 2 A3
Church St. Hors DE21 .... 22 C3
Church St. Ilk DE7 .... 25 C2

Church St. Kilb DE56 .... 22 C4
Church St. Ripley DE5 .... 10 B1
Church St. Ripley DE5 .... 17 A4
Church St. Som DE55 .... 11 B3
Church St. Tans DE4 .... 1 A2
Church St. Wirk DE4 .... 6 C4
Church View. Hean DE75 ...... 17 A2
Church Wlk. Brin NG16 .... 18 C4
Church Wlk. Duff DE56 .... 21 C1
Church Wlk. East NG16 .... 18 C1
Church Wlk. Som DE55 .... 11 C3
Cinder Bank. Iron NG16 .... 11 C2
Cinder La. Wirk DE4 .... 6 C3
Cinder Rd. Som DE55 .... 11 B4
Clara Mount Rd. Hean DE75 .. 18 A1
Clarke Ave. Hean DE75 .... 17 B1
Claxton Cl. Hean DE75 .... 17 B1
Claxton Terr. Hean DE75 .... 17 B1
Clay La. Hean DE75 .... 17 C1
Clayton Gr. Hean DE75 .... 17 B2
Clement Rd. H Wood DE7 ...... 23 B4
Cliffash La. Idri DE56 .... 12 C3
Clifton Dr. Derby DE3 .... 29 C2
Clifton Rd. Derby DE22 .... 28 C2
Clinton Ave. Brin NG16 .... 18 B3
Close The. Derby DE23 .... 28 C1
Clover Nook Ind Est. S Norm ....
DE55 .... 5 C2
Clover Nook Rd. Pinx DE55 .... 5 C2
Clover Nook Rd. Som DE55 .... 5 C2
Clover Nook Rd. S Norm DE55 5 C2
Cloves Hill. Morley DE7 .... 23 B3
Cloves Hill. Smal DE7 .... 23 B1
Clumber Ct. Ilk DE7 .... 25 C3
Cluster Rd. Belper DE56 .... 14 C2
Clusters The. Belper DE56 .... 14 C2
Coach Dr. East NG16 .... 18 C2
Coach Dr. Quar DE22 .... 28 B4
Coach Rd. Iron DE5 .... 11 B2
Coach Rd. Iron NG16 .... 11 B2
Coach Rd. Ripley DE5 .... 10 C2
Coach Rd. Som DE55 .... 11 B2
Coachways. Mapp DE7 .... 24 C2
Coasthill. Crich DE4 .... 2 C1
Cobden St. Ripley DE5 .... 10 B1
Cobthorn Dr. Derby DE22 ...... 28 B2
Cockerhouse Rd. East NG16 .. 18 C2
Cockshutt La. Som DE55 ...... 11 C4
Codnor CE Prim Sch. Codnor ....
DE5 .... 17 A4
Codnor Denby La. Codnor DE5 17 A3
Codnor Denby La. Denby DE5 17 A3
Codnor Gate. Codnor DE5 ..... 11 A1
Codnor Gate Ind Est. Ripley ....
DE5 .... 11 A1
Codnor La. Som DE5 .... 11 B1
Coffin La. K Ire DE6 .... 6 A1
Colin Ave. Codnor DE5 .... 17 A4
Colin St. Alf DE55 .... 5 A2
Colledge St. Som DE55 .... 11 B3
Colliery Row. Alf DE55 .... 5 A3
Common The. Crich DE4 .... 9 A4
Common The. Quar DE22 ...... 28 B4
Connaught Ct. Alf DE55 .... 5 A2
Cook Cl. Belper DE56 .... 15 C3
Cookfield. Heage DE56 .... 15 C4
Cookham Cl. Derby DE3 .... 29 B1
Cooper St. Ripley DE5 .... 10 B1
Copper Yd. Denby DE5 .... 16 C1
Coppice Ave. Ilk DE7 .... 25 B3
Coppice Cl. Derby DE22 .... 28 C1
Coppice Cl. Kilb DE56 .... 23 A4
Coppice Dr. East NG16 .... 18 B2
Coppice Dr. Hean DE75 .... 24 C4
Coppice Prim Sch. Hean DE75 24 C4
Copse Cl. Wirk DE4 .... 6 C4
Copse The. Ilk DE7 .... 25 B3
Copthorne Inf Sch. Alf DE55 ... 5 A3
Cordy La. Brin NG16 .... 18 C4
Cordy La. Sels NG16 .... 18 C4
Corfield Ave. Hean DE75 .... 24 C4
Cornfield CE Inf Sch. Hean ....
DE75 .... 17 B1
Cornhill. Derby DE22 .... 28 C2

Cornhill Ct. Alf DE55 .... 5 A2
Cornhill Dr. Alf DE55 .... 5 A2
Coronation Ave. Belper DE56 . 15 A3
Coronation Rd. Mapp DE7 ..... 24 C2
Cotes Park Ind Est. Alf DE55 ... 5 B1
Cotes Park La. Som DE55 ...... 5 B1
Cotmanhay Inf & Jun Sch. Ilk ....
DE7 .... 25 C3
Cotmanhay Rd. Ilk DE7 .... 25 C2
Cottage Cl. Ilk DE7 .... 25 B2
Cottage Garden La. Hean ....
DE75 .... 17 B1
Coupe St. Ripley DE5 .... 16 C4
Coupland Pl. Som DE55 .... 5 B1
Courtney Way. Belper DE56 ... 15 B3
Cowham Cl. Alf DE55 .... 5 B2
Coxbench Rd. Hors DE21 ...... 22 C2
Crabtree Cl. Derby DE22 .... 28 B2
Crabtree Cl. Wirk DE4 .... 6 C4
Crabtree Hill. Derby DE21 ..... 28 B2
Cranmer St. Ilk DE7 .... 25 C1
Cray's Hill. Swan DE55 .... 11 A4
Crescent The. Alf DE55 .... 5 A2
Crescent The. H Wood DE7 ... 23 B4
Cressy Rd. Alf DE55 .... 5 A2
Crest The. Derby DE22 .... 28 C1
Crich Carr CE Prim Sch. Crich ....
DE4 .... 2 B1
Crich CE Inf Sch. Crich DE4 ... 2 C1
Crich Dr. Heage DE56 .... 15 C4
Crich Jun Sch. Crich DE4 .... 3 A1
Crich La. Belper DE56 .... 15 A4
Crich La. Ridge DE56 .... 9 A2
Crich Rd. Fritch DE56 .... 9 A3
Critchley St. Ilk DE7 .... 25 C1
Croft Inf Sch. Alf DE55 .... 5 A2
Croft The. Belper DE56 .... 15 B1
Croft The. Heage DE56 .... 9 C1
Croft The. Morley DE7 .... 23 B1
Croft The. Som DE55 .... 11 B4
Cromer Cl. Derby DE3 .... 29 B1
Cromford Cl. Ald NG16 .... 18 A2
Cromford Dr. Derby DE3 .... 29 C2
Cromford Rd. Ald NG16 .... 17 C3
Cromford Rd. Crich DE4 .... 2 C1
Cromford Rd. La Mill NG16 ... 18 A2
Cromford Rd. Ripley DE5 ...... 10 B1
Cromwell Dr. Swan DE55 ...... 10 B4
Cross La. Codnor DE5 .... 17 A4
Cross La. Shirl DE55 .... 4 C4
Cross La. Wess DE55 .... 3 C4
Cross Lanes. Hollow DE4 .... 1 B1
Crosshill. Codnor DE5 .... 17 A3
Crossley St. Ripley DE5 .... 10 B1
Crossways La. H Ward DE6 ... 12 A1
Crown St. Duff DE56 .... 21 C2
Crown Terr. Belper DE56 .... 14 C2
Croydon Wlk. Derby DE22 ..... 29 C3
Culland View. Crich DE4 .... 9 A4
Culworth Cl. Belper DE56 ...... 15 B2
Cumberhills Rd. Duff DE56 .... 21 B1
Cumbria Wlk. Derby DE3 ...... 29 B1
Cunnery La. Tans DE4 .... 1 A2
Cunnery The. K Lang DE6 ..... 26 C1
Curzon CE Prim Sch The. Quar ....
DE22 .... 28 B3
Curzon Cl. Derby DE22 .... 28 B2
Curzon Ct. Duff DE56 .... 21 C2
Curzon La. Duff DE56 .... 21 B2

D H Lawrence Mus. East NG16 ....
.... 18 C2
Dale Ave. Som DE55 .... 11 B3
Dale Cl. Fritch DE56 .... 9 A3
Dale Ct. Kilb DE56 .... 22 C4
Dale Park Ave. Kilb DE56 ...... 23 A4
Dale View Gdns. Kilb DE56 ... 22 C4
Dalley La. Belper DE56 .... 14 B3
Daltons Cl. Ald NG16 .... 18 A2
Danesby Cres. Denby DE5 .... 16 A1
Danesby Rise. Denby DE5 ..... 16 A1
Dannah Cres. Ripley DE5 ...... 10 C1
Dannah St. Ripley DE5 .... 10 C1

Darfield Dr. Hean DE75 .... 18 A1
Dark La. Callow DE4 .... 6 B2
Dark La. Crich DE4 .... 2 C3
Dark La. Holbr DE56 .... 22 A4
Darley Abbey Dr. Derby DE22 28 C1
Darley Dr. Ripley DE5 .... 10 B2
Darley Park Dr. Derby DE22 .. 28 C1
Darley Park Rd. Derby DE22 .. 28 C1
Darley Sq. Ilk DE7 .... 25 C3
Darwin Rd. Derby DE3 .... 29 C2
Daventry Cl. Derby DE3 .... 29 B2
Dawlish Ct. East NG16 .... 18 B2
Days La. Belper DE56 .... 14 C2
Deacon Cl. Swan DE55 .... 10 C4
Dean Rd. Toad DE56 .... 8 C1
Dean St. La Mill NG16 .... 18 B2
Deepdale. Iron NG16 .... 11 C2
Deepdale Ct. Hean DE75 .... 17 C1
Deepdale Rd. Belper DE56 ..... 15 A3
Delamere Cl. Swan DE55 ...... 10 C4
Delves Bank Rd. Swan DE55 . 11 A4
Delves Rd. Hean DE75 .... 24 B4
Delves Rd. Ship DE75 .... 24 B4
Delves Specl Sch. Swan DE55
.... 10 C4
Delves The. Swan DE55 .... 10 C4
Denby Comm. Denby DE5 ...... 16 C2
Denby Free CE Prim Sch. Denby
DE5 .... 16 B1
Denby La. Denby DE5 .... 16 B1
Denton Way. Swan DE55 .... 10 C4
Denver Rd. Derby DE3 .... 29 B2
Derby Rd. Alder DE56 .... 8 C1
Derby Rd. Alf DE55 .... 4 C2
Derby Rd. Amber DE56 .... 8 C2
Derby Rd. Belper DE56 .... 21 C4
Derby Rd. Denby DE5 .... 16 B2
Derby Rd. Duff DE56 .... 21 C1
Derby Rd. East NG16 .... 18 C1
Derby Rd. Hean DE75 .... 17 B1
Derby Rd. Hors DE21 .... 22 B3
Derby Rd. Kilb DE56 .... 15 C1
Derby Rd. La Mill NG16 .... 18 B2
Derby Rd. Ripley DE5 .... 10 B2
Derby Rd. Swan DE5, DE55 ... 10 C3
Derby Rd. Wirk DE4 .... 6 C3
Derby Road Ind Est. Hean
DE75 .... 17 B1
Derby Univ (Mickleover Site).
Derby DE3 .... 29 C2
Derwent Ave. Belper DE56 ..... 15 A1
Derwent Ave. Ilk DE7 .... 25 B1
Derwent Gr. Alf DE55 .... 4 C1
Derwent Rd. Ripley DE5 .... 10 B1
Derwent St. Belper DE56 .... 14 C2
Derwent Vale. Belper DE56 .... 14 C1
Derwent Valley Visitor Ctr. Belper
DE56 .... 14 C3
Derwent View. Belper DE56 ... 14 C3
Dethick La. Hollow DE4 .... 1 B1
Devonshire Ave. Derby DE22 . 28 C2
Devonshire Cl. Ilk DE7 .... 25 C3
Devonshire Dr. Derby DE3 ..... 29 C2
Devonshire Dr. Duff DE56 ...... 21 B1
Devonshire Dr. East NG16 ..... 18 C1
Devonshire Dr. Som DE55 ..... 11 A4
Devonshire St. Toad DE56 ...... 8 C2
Dewy La. Ash DE4 .... 1 C1
Dewy La. Crich DE4 .... 1 C1
Dimple La. Crich DE4 .... 9 A4
Dix Ave. Smal DE7 .... 23 C3
Dobholes La. Smal DE7 .... 23 C3
Dodford Ct. Hean DE75 .... 18 A1
Doehole La. Ash DE4 .... 1 C2
Donald Hawley Way. Duff
DE56 .... 21 C2
Donner Cres. Ilk DE7 .... 25 C3
Douglas Ave. Hean DE75 .... 17 B1
Douglas Rd. Som DE55 .... 11 B4
Dove Cl. Kilb DE56 .... 23 A4
Dove Rd. Ripley DE5 .... 10 B1
Dovecote The. Hors DE21 ...... 22 C3
Dovedale Cir. Ilk DE7 .... 25 C3
Dovedale Cl. Ripley DE5 .... 16 B3

Dovedale Cres. Belper DE56 .. 15 A3
Dovedale Ct. Belper DE56 ...... 15 A2
Dovedale Rise. Derby DE22 ... 28 B1
Downham Cl. Derby DE3 .... 29 C1
Downing Cl. Derby DE22 .... 29 C3
Downmeadow. Heage DE56 ... 15 C4
Draycott Cl. Hean DE75 .... 17 B2
Draycott Ct. Ilk DE7 .... 25 C2
Draycott Dr. Derby DE3 .... 29 B2
Drayton Ave. Derby DE22 ...... 29 C3
Dresden Cl. Derby DE3 .... 29 B1
Drive The. Haz DE56 .... 13 C2
Dronfield Pl. Ilk DE7 .... 25 C3
Drovers Way. Bullbr DE56 .... 9 A3
Drummond Rd. Ilk DE7 .... 25 C1
Drysdale Rd. Derby DE3 .... 29 B2
Duffield Bank. Duff DE56 .... 22 A2
Duffield Rd. Derby DE22 .... 28 C1
Duffield Sta. Duff DE56 .... 21 C2
Duke St. Ilk DE7 .... 25 C2
Dukes Pl. Ilk DE7 .... 25 C2
Dulwich Rd. Derby DE22 .... 29 C3
Dumbles La. Denby DE5 .... 16 C1
Duncan Cl. Belper DE56 .... 15 A3
Dunedin Cl. Derby DE3 .... 29 C2
Dungley Hill. Heage DE56 .... 9 B1
Dunsford Rd. Alf DE55 .... 5 A3
Durham St. Ilk DE7 .... 25 C1

Each Well La. Alf DE55 .... 4 C2
Eagle St. Heage DE56 .... 9 C1
Earlswood Dr. Derby DE3 ...... 29 C2
East Ave. Derby DE3 .... 29 C2
East Cl. Derby DE22 .... 28 C1
East Cres. Holbr DE56 .... 22 B4
East Nelson St. Hean DE75 .... 17 C1
East St. Hean DE75 .... 25 A4
East View Rd. Heage DE56 ...... 9 C1
Eastfield Rd. Ripley DE5 .... 11 A1
Eastleigh Dr. Derby DE3 .... 29 C1
Eastwood Comp Sch. East
NG16 .... 18 C2
Eastwood Jun & Inf Schs. East
NG16 .... 18 C2
Eaton Bank. Lit Ea DE56 .... 22 A1
Eaton Ct. Duff DE56 .... 21 C1
Ebenezer St. Ilk DE7 .... 25 C2
Ebenezer St. La Mill NG16 .... 18 A2
Ecclesbourne Ave. Duff DE56 21 C2
Ecclesbourne Cl. Duff DE56 .. 21 C2
Ecclesbourne Cl. Wirk DE4 ..... 6 C4
Ecclesbourne La. Idri DE56 ... 12 C3
Ecclesbourne Sch. Duff DE56 21 C2
Edale Ave. Derby DE3 .... 29 B1
Edale Cl. Derby DE22 .... 28 B1
Edale Sq. Ilk DE7 .... 25 C3
Edale Way. Belper DE56 .... 15 A3
Eden Bank. Toad DE56 .... 8 C1
Edensor Dr. Belper DE56 .... 15 B3
Edgware Rd. Derby DE22 .... 29 C3
Edinburgh Ct. Swan DE55 ..... 11 A4
Edward St. Ald NG16 .... 18 A2
Edward St. Belper DE56 .... 15 A2
Edwards Cres. Kilb DE56 .... 23 A4
Egreaves Ave. Hean DE75 ..... 17 B2
Elder Cl. Swan DE55 .... 11 A4
Eley Cl. Ilk DE7 .... 25 B1
Elizabeth Ct. Ilk DE7 .... 25 B1
Elizabeth Pk. Iron NG16 .... 11 C3
Ella Bank Rd. Hean DE75 ...... 18 A1
Ellesmere Ave. Alf DE55 .... 5 A2
Elm Ave. Belper DE56 .... 15 A1
Elm Gr. Derby DE22 .... 28 B3
Elm Tree Ave. Kilb DE56 .... 23 A4
Elms Ave. Alf DE55 .... 5 A2
Elms Ave. Ripley DE5 .... 16 B4
Elms Cl. Alf DE55 .... 5 A2
Elmsfield Ave. Hean DE75 ..... 18 A1
Elmwood Dr. Alf DE55 .... 5 B2
Elnor St. La Mill NG16 .... 18 B2
Elsecar Cl. Belper DE56 .... 15 B3
Elveden Dr. Ilk DE7 .... 25 B2
Embankment Cl. Derby DE22 . 29 C4

Emmas Williams Ct. Ripley
DE5 .... 10 B1
Emsworth Cl. Ship DE7 .... 25 B2
Endsleigh Gdns. Derby DE22 . 29 C3
England Cres. Hean DE75 ...... 18 A1
Epping Cl. Derby DE22 .... 29 C3
Erewash Ct. Ilk DE7 .... 25 B1
Essex St. Ilk DE7 .... 25 C1
Estwic Ave. East NG16 .... 18 C2
Etwall Rd. Derby DE3 .... 29 B1
Everest Dr. Som DE55 .... 11 B4
Ewart La. Alf DE55 .... 4 C2
Eyam Wlk. Belper DE56 .... 15 A3
Eyes Ct. Duff DE56 .... 21 C2
Eyre's Gdns. Ilk DE7 .... 25 C1

Factory La. Ilk DE7 .... 25 C1
Fairbourne Dr. Derby DE3 ..... 29 B2
Fairfield Rd. H Wood DE7 ...... 23 B4
Fairview Cl. Kilb DE56 .... 23 A4
Fairview Grange. Kilb DE56 ... 23 A4
Fairview Rise. Fritch DE4 .... 9 A4
Fairway Cl. Derby DE22 .... 28 B1
Fairway Cres. Derby DE22 ..... 28 B1
Falcon Ct. Ilk DE7 .... 25 B1
Falcons Rise. Belper DE56 .... 15 B3
Fall Rd. Hean DE75 .... 17 C2
Far Laund. Belper DE56 .... 15 A3
Farm Cl. Belper DE56 .... 15 B2
Farm Cl. Kilb DE56 .... 23 A4
Farm Cl. Pent DE5 .... 10 A3
Farm Cl. Som DE55 .... 11 B4
Farnah Green Rd. Belper DE56 14 B2
Farneworth Rd. Derby DE3 .... 29 B1
Farnham Cl. Derby DE3 .... 29 B1
Farnway. Derby DE22 .... 28 C1
Farriers Croft. Ilk DE7 .... 25 B2
Farringdon Cl. Derby DE22 .... 29 C3
Fearn Ave. Ripley DE5 .... 10 C1
Fellside. Belper DE56 .... 15 A2
Fenton Rd. Derby DE3 .... 29 B1
Fern Cres. East NG16 .... 18 B2
Ferrers Cres. Duff DE56 .... 21 B2
Ferrers Way. Derby DE22 .... 28 C1
Ferrers Way. Ripley DE5 .... 10 B2
Field Ct. Kilb DE56 .... 23 A4
Field La. Belper DE56 .... 14 C2
Field La. K Ire DE56 .... 12 A4
Field Row. Belper DE56 .... 14 C2
Field St. Codnor DE5 .... 17 A4
Field Terr. Ripley DE5 .... 10 B1
Field The. Ship DE75 .... 25 A3
Fieldon Cl. K Lang DE6 .... 26 C1
Finchley Ave. Derby DE22 ..... 29 C3
Findern Cl. Belper DE56 .... 15 B3
Findern Cl. Derby DE22 .... 28 B1
Finningley Dr. Derby DE22 ..... 28 C1
Firestone. Haz DE56 .... 14 B1
Firlawns. Duff DE56 .... 21 B2
Firs Ave. Alf DE55 .... 5 A3
Firs Ave. Ripley DE5 .... 10 B1
Firs Cres. Derby DE22 .... 28 C2
Firs Gdns. Alf DE55 .... 5 A2
Fisher Cl. Ilk DE7 .... 25 C2
Fisher La. Duff DE56 .... 21 C2
Flagshaw La. K Lang DE6 ...... 26 C2
Flamstead Ave. Hean DE75 ... 17 B2
Flamstead La. Denby DE5 ...... 16 C1
Flamstead Rd. Ilk DE7 .... 25 C1
Flat The. Kilb DE56 .... 22 C4
Flaxholme Ave. Duff DE56 ..... 21 C1
Fleet Cres. Belper DE56 .... 14 C2
Fleet Pk. Belper DE56 .... 15 A2
Fleet The. Belper DE56 .... 14 C2
Fletcher St. Hean DE75 .... 17 C1
Fletcher's Row. Ripley DE5 .... 10 C1
Florence Ct. Ilk DE7 .... 25 C1
Flowery Leys La. Alf DE55 .... 5 B2
Foggs Entry. Wirk DE4 .... 6 C4
Folds Yd. Crich DE4 .... 2 C1
Ford Ave. Hean DE75 .... 17 B2
Ford Cl. Ripley DE5 .... 16 B4
Ford St. Belper DE56 .... 14 C2

Forest Cl. Belper DE56 .... 15 A3
Foresters Way. Ripley DE5 ..... 10 B1
Forty Horse Cl. Ripley DE5 ..... 11 A1
Foundry La. Belper DE56 .... 21 C4
Foxes Wlk. Derby DE22 .... 28 C2
Foxholes La. Tans DE4 .... 1 A4
Foxlands Ave. Derby DE22 ..... 28 C1
Frederic Ave. Hean DE75 .... 24 C4
Frederick St. Alf DE55 .... 5 A3
Frederick St. Som DE55 .... 11 B3
Freemantle Rd. Derby DE3 .... 29 C2
Freesia Cl. Derby DE3 .... 29 C1
French La. Hors DE21 .... 22 C3
Fritchley CE Prim Sch. Fritch
DE56 .... 9 A3
Fritchley La. Crich DE56 .... 9 A4
Froggett Cl. Som DE55 .... 11 B4
Front St. Fritch DE56 .... 9 A3
Frost Ave. La Mill NG16 .... 18 A2
Fryar Rd. East NG16 .... 18 C2
Fullwood Ave. Ilk DE7 .... 25 C1
Fullwood St. Ilk DE7 .... 25 C1
Furnace La. Hean DE75 .... 17 B2
Furnace Row. Som DE55 .... 11 C4

Gadsby Rise. N Heage DE56 .... 9 B1
Garden Cr. S Norm DE55 .... 5 C2
Garden Rd. East NG16 .... 18 C2
Gardens The. Hean DE75 ...... 17 B2
Gardens The. Ripley DE5 .... 16 B4
Garner La. S Wing DE4, DE55 . 3 B1
Garnett Ave. Hean DE75 .... 17 C1
Gate Brook Cl. Codnor DE5 ... 11 A1
George Cres. Som DE55 .... 11 B3
George St. Alf DE55 .... 5 A2
George St. Belper DE56 .... 14 C2
George St. La Mill NG16 .... 18 A2
George St. Ridd DE55 .... 11 B3
George St. Som DE55 .... 11 B4
George St. S Norm DE55 .... 5 C3
Gibfield La. Belper DE56 .... 14 C1
Gilbert Cres. Duff DE56 .... 21 C1
Gillot St. Hean DE75 .... 25 A4
Gimson Cl. Ilk DE7 .... 25 B2
Gin La. Ash S45 .... 1 C4
Gisborne Cl. Derby DE3 .... 29 C2
Gisborne Cres. Derby DE22 ... 28 C2
Gladstone Ave. Hean DE75 .... 17 C1
Gladstone Dr. Brin NG16 .... 18 C4
Gladstone Rd. Alf DE55 .... 4 C2
Gladstone St. Hean DE75 ...... 17 C1
Gladstone St. La Mill NG16 ... 18 B2
Glasshouse Hill. Codnor DE5 17 A4
Glebe Ave. Ripley DE5 .... 10 B1
Glebe Ave. Smal DE7 .... 23 C3
Glen Ave. Holbr DE56 .... 22 B4
Glen Rd. Crich DE4 .... 2 B1
Glen View. Belper DE56 .... 14 C1
Glen Vine. Ripley DE5 .... 11 A1
Glendon St. Stanl DE7 .... 24 A1
Gleneagles Cl. Derby DE3 ..... 29 C1
Glenfield Cres. Derby DE3 ..... 29 B1
Godfrey St. Hean DE75 .... 17 C1
Godkin Dr. Ald NG16 .... 18 A2
Gold La. Mack DE22 .... 29 C4
Golden Valley. H Wood DE7 ... 23 A3
Golden Valley. Som DE55 ...... 11 B2
Goldhill. Tans DE4 .... 1 A2
Golf La. Duff DE56 .... 21 C3
Goods Rd. Belper DE56 .... 14 C1
Goods Yd. Belper DE56 .... 14 C1
Goodwin's La. Haz DE56 .... 14 B1
Gooker La. Alf DE55 .... 4 C2
Goose La. Codnor DE5 .... 17 B4
Gordon Rd. Swan DE55 .... 10 C4
Gorses. Alder DE56 .... 14 B4
Gorses. Idri DE56 .... 12 B3
Gorsey Bank. Wirk DE4 .... 6 C4
Gorsey Cl. Belper DE56 .... 14 C3
Gorsey La. K Ire DE6 .... 6 A1
Grace Cres. Hean DE75 .... 17 C1
Grammer St. Hean DE5 .... 17 A2
Granby Jun Sch. Ilk DE7 .... 25 C2

Granby St. Ilk DE7 25 C1
Grandfield St. Hean DE75 17 B2
Grange Cl. Som DE55 5 C1
Grange St. Alf DE55 5 A2
Grange The. Smal DE75 24 B4
Grange View. East NG16 18 C2
Grangewood Dr. Belper DE56 22 A4
Grant Way. East NG16 18 C2
Granville Cl. Duff DE56 21 C2
Grass St. Ilk DE7 25 C2
Grayswood Cl. Swan DE55 11 A4
Great Northern Rd. East NG16 18 B1
Greaves St. Ripley DE5 10 C1
Green La. Belper DE56 14 C2
Green La. Tans DE4 1 A3
Green La. W Und DE6 19 C1
Green The. Alf DE55 5 A2
Green The. Belper DE56 15 A3
Green The. Derby DE22 28 B1
Green The. Derby DE74 29 B1
Green The. Fritch DE56 9 A3
Green The. K Lang DE6 26 B1
Green The. Swan DE55 10 C4
Greenacre Ave. Hean DE75 18 A2
Greenfields. Ald NG16 18 A2
Greenfields. Fritch DE4 9 A4
Greenhill Ave. Ripley DE5 16 C4
Greenhill Ind Est. Som DE55 11 A3
Greenhill La. Som DE55 11 B3
Greenhills Rd. East NG16 18 C2
Greens Ct. Ilk DE7 25 B1
Greenside Ct. Derby DE3 29 B1
Gregg Ave. Hean DE75 17 C1
Gregory Ave. Ald NG16 18 A2
Gregory Ave. La Mill NG16 18 A2
Gregory St. Ilk DE7 25 C1
Gregorys Way. Belper DE56 15 B3
Grendon Cl. Belper DE56 15 A3
Grenville Dr. Ilk DE7 25 C2
Grenvoir Dr. Ripley DE5 11 A1
Gresley Rd. Ilk DE7 25 C1
Griggs Gdns. Wirk DE4 6 C4
Groome Ave. Hean DE75 17 B2
Grosvenor Rd. East NG16 18 C1
Grosvenor Rd. Ripley DE5 10 B1
Grove Ct. Ripley DE5 16 C4
Grove Mews. East NG16 18 C1
Grove The. Derby DE72 29 C1
Guide Post. N Heage DE56 9 B1
Gun La. N Heage DE56 9 B1
Gunhills La. Wind DE56 20 C3

Haddon Cl. Alf DE55 4 C2
Haddon Cl. Bullbr DE56 9 A3
Haddon Cl. Derby DE22 28 B2
Haddon Dr. Derby DE3 28 B2
Haddon Dr. Derby DE3 29 C2
Haddon Dr. Lit Ea DE21 22 B1
Haddon Nurseries. Ilk DE7 25 C2
Haddon St. Ilk DE7 25 C2
Hagg La. Wind DE56 13 B1
Hailsham Cl. Derby DE3 29 B2
Halfmoon La. Callow DE6 6 A2
Halfmoon La. K Ire DE4 6 A2
Hall Farm Rd. Duff DE56 21 C1
Hall La. Brai DE6 26 A3
Hall La. Brin NG16 18 B3
Hall La. N Heage DE56 9 B2
Hall Rd. Ald NG16 18 B2
Hall St. Alf DE55 5 A2
Hallington Dr. Hean DE75 17 B1
Hallum Ct. Ilk DE7 25 C2
Hamilton Cl. Derby DE3 29 C2
Hamlet The. Hean DE75 17 C2
Hammersmith. Ripley DE5 10 B2
Hammonds Ct. Wirk DE4 6 C4
Hand's Rd. Hean DE75 18 A1
Hardwick Ave. Derby DE22 28 B2
Hardwick Cl. Ripley DE5 10 B2
Hardwick Dr. Derby DE3 29 C1
Hardy Barn. Ship DE75 25 A4
Hardy Cres. Codnor DE5 17 A4
Hardy St. Alf DE55 4 C3
Harewood Rd. Derby DE22 28 B2
Harlech Cl. Ilk DE7 25 B2
Harlequin Ct. East NG16 18 B2
Harold Ave. Ald NG16 18 A2
Harpole Cl. Swan DE55 10 C4
Harpswell Cl. Derby DE22 28 C1
Harrier Rd. Belper DE56 15 B3
Harris Ave. Ripley DE5 10 B1
Harris Cl. Ripley DE5 10 B1
Hartington Pl. Ilk DE7 25 C3
Hartington Way. Derby DE3 29 B1
Hartshay Hill. Ripley DE5 10 B1
Hassock La N. Ship DE75 25 A4
Hassock La S. Ship DE75 25 B3
Haston Dr. Som DE55 11 B4
Hathersage Dr. Som DE55 11 A4
Havelock St. Ripley DE5 10 C1
Hawkins Ct. Ilk DE7 25 C2
Hawkins Dr. Ridge DE56 9 A2
Hawthorn Ave. Ripley DE5 16 B4
Hawthorne Cl. Kilb DE56 15 C1
Hawthornes Ave. S Norm DE55 5 C3
Hawthorns The. Belper DE56 15 B3
Hay La. Spout DE56 7 B3
Hay La. Wirk DE56 7 B3
Hayes Con Ctr The. Swan DE55 11 A3
Hayes Cres. Swan DE55 10 C4
Hayes La. Swan DE55 10 C4
Hayes Wood Rd. Stanl DE7 24 A1
Hayfield Cl. Belper DE56 15 A3
Hayley Croft. Duff DE56 21 C1
Hayling Cl. Ship DE7 25 B2
Hays Cl. Ilk DE7 25 B1
Hazel Cl. Hean DE75 17 B1
Hazel Gr. Duff DE56 21 C2
Hazeldene Cl. Duff DE56 21 C3
Hazeltree Cl. Ripley DE5 16 B4
Hazelwood Hill. Haz DE56 21 B4
Hazelwood Rd. Duff DE56 21 B3
Hazelwood Rd. Haz DE56 21 B3
Heage Prim Sch. Heage DE56 9 B1
Heage Rd. Ripley DE5 10 B1
Heanor Gate Ind Est. Hean DE75 24 B4
Heanor Gate Rd. Hean DE75 24 B4
Heanor Gate Rd. Ship DE75 24 B4
Heanor Gate Sch. Hean DE75 17 B1
Heanor Langley Mill & District Meml Hospl. Hean DE75 17 C1
Heanor Rd. Codnor DE5 17 A4
Heanor Rd. Denby DE5 17 A2
Heanor Rd. Hean DE75 17 B1
Heanor Rd. Hean DE75 17 B2
Heanor Rd. Ilk DE7 25 B2
Heanor Rd. Smal DE7 24 A4
Heath Rd. Ripley DE5 10 C1
Heather Cl. Swan DE55 11 A4
Heavygate La. Shot DE56 13 C4
Hedley Cl. Som DE55 11 B4
Hemp Yd. K Ire DE6 6 A1
Hemsley Dr. East NG16 18 B2
Henley Gn. Derby DE22 29 C3
Henry Cres. Alf DE55 5 B2
Henry St. Ripley DE5 10 B1
Henshaw Pl. Ilk DE7 25 C2
Herbert Strutt Prim Sch. Belper DE56 14 C1
Hermitage Ave. Som DE55 11 B3
Heydon Cl. Belper DE56 15 A3
Heyford Ct. Hean DE75 18 A1
Hickleton Cl. Ripley DE5 10 B1
Hickton Rd. Swan DE55 10 C3
Higg La. Alder DE4, DE56 8 A3
High Bank. Denby DE5 16 C1
High Edge Dr. Heage DE56 15 C4
High Edge Mews. Belper DE56 15 A3
High Holborn. Ilk DE7 25 C2
High Holborn Rd. Codnor DE5 11 A1
High Holborn Rd. Ripley DE5 11 A1
High La. Hollow DE4 1 C1
High La. Hollow DE4 2 B3
High La Central. We Ha DE7 24 C1
High La W. We Ha DE7 24 C1
High Meadow Cl. Ripley DE5 16 B4
High Pavement. Belper DE56 15 A2
High Rd. S Wing DE55 3 C2
High St. Alf DE55 5 A2
High St. Belper DE56 15 A2
High St. Codnor DE5 17 A4
High St. Hean DE75 17 B2
High St. Hean DE75 17 C1
High St. Kilb DE56 23 A4
High St. Ridd DE55 11 B3
High St. Ripley DE5 10 B1
High St. Som DE55 11 B4
High St. Swan DE55 10 C4
Highbury Cl. Derby DE22 29 C3
Highfield Cl. Hean DE75 17 A3
Highfield La. W Und DE6 19 C3
Highfield Rd. Belper DE56 14 C1
Highfield Rd. Kilb DE56 22 C4
Highfield Rd. Swan DE55 10 B4
Highfield Way. Ripley DE5 16 B4
Highfields. Codnor DE5 17 A4
Highgate Dr. Ship DE7 25 B2
Highgrove Cl. Hean DE75 17 B1
Highwood Ave. Belper DE56 15 B1
Hilary Cl. Belper DE56 15 C3
Hill Cl. Stanl DE7 24 A1
Hill Cl. Turn DE56 13 A1
Hill Crest. Crich DE4 3 A1
Hill Rd. Hean DE75 17 B1
Hill St. Ripley DE5 10 B2
Hill Top La. Kilb DE56 15 C1
Hill Top Rd. Som DE55 11 B3
Hill View. Duff DE56 21 B2
Hill View Cl. H Wood DE7 23 A4
Hillberry. Ripley DE5 11 A1
Hillcliff La. H Ward DE56 12 C1
Hillcrest Dr. Codnor DE5 17 A4
Hillcrest Dr. Kilb DE56 23 A4
Hillside. Hollow DE4 2 A3
Hillside. La Mill NG16 18 A2
Hillside Rise. Belper DE56 14 C1
Hilltop. Fritch DE56 9 A4
Hilton Cl. Derby DE3 29 B1
Hilton Park Dr. Som DE55 11 B4
Hindersitch La. Crich DE4 2 B1
Hindscarth Cres. Derby DE3 29 C1
Hob Hill. Haz DE56 21 A4
Hob La. K Ire DE56 12 B4
Hobart Cl. Derby DE3 29 C1
Hobsic Cl. Brin NG16 18 B4
Hockley Way. Som DE55 5 A1
Hoggbarn La. Hean NG16 17 B3
Hoggs Field. East NG16 18 C1
Holborn View. Codnor DE5 11 A1
Holbrook CE Prim Sch. Holbr DE56 22 B4
Holbrook Rd. Belper DE56 14 C1
Holbrook St. Hean DE75 18 A1
Holbrook View. Kilb DE56 23 A4
Holkham Cl. Ship DE7 25 B2
Hollies Rd. Derby DE22 28 B2
Hollies The. East NG16 18 C1
Hollins La. Crich DE4 3 A2
Hollins The. Hollow DE4 2 A3
Hollins Wood Cl. Hollow DE4 2 A3
Hollow The. Hollow DE4 2 A3
Holloway Rd. Duff DE56 21 C2
Holly Ave. Ripley DE5 16 B4
Holly Bank Cl. S Wing DE55 4 A2
Holly Bush La. Belper DE56 22 A3
Holly Ct. Derby DE3 29 B1
Holly Gr. Swan DE55 10 C4
Holly La. Alder DE56 8 B2
Holly La. Tans DE4 1 A2
Hollyhurst Row. Som DE55 11 C3
Hollywell Ave. Codnor DE5 17 A4
Holm La. S Wing DE55 4 A2
Holme Cl. Hollow DE4 2 A3
Holme Cl. Ilk DE7 25 B1
Holmes Cl. La Mill NG16 18 A2
Holmes St. Hean DE75 17 B1
Holmesfield Cl. Tans DE4 1 A3
Holmesfield Dr. Derby DE3 29 C1
Holmesfield Dr. Ship DE75 25 A4
Holt La. Hollow DE4 2 A4
Holywell Rd. Ship DE7 25 B2
Homestead. Ald NG16 18 A2
Honeycroft Cl. Belper DE56 15 A1
Honeyfield Dr. Ripley DE5 16 C4
Honingham Rd. Ilk DE7 25 B2
Hope Ave. Derby DE3 29 B1
Hopewell Wlk. Ilk DE7 25 C3
Hopkins Ct. East NG16 18 C2
Hopping Hill. Belper DE56 21 C4
Hopping Hill Terr E. Belper DE56 22 A4
Hopping Hill Terr W. Belper DE56 22 A4
Horeston Cotts. H Wood DE7 23 A4
Horridge St. Ilk DE7 25 C2
Horsecroft Cl. Ilk DE7 25 B1
Horsley CE Prim Sch. Hors DE21 22 C3
Horsley Cres. Holbr DE56 22 B4
Horsley Cres. La Mill NG16 18 A2
Horsley La. Hors DE21 22 C2
Horsley Rd. Hors DE21 22 C3
Horsley Rd. Kilb DE56 22 C3
Horsley Woodhouse Prim Sch. H Wood DE7 23 B3
Horton Cl. Swan DE55 10 C4
Houghton Ave. Ilk DE7 25 B2
Howden Cl. Derby DE3 29 B1
Howitt St. Hean DE75 17 C1
Hoylake Ct. Derby DE3 29 B2
Hoylake Dr. Derby DE3 29 B2
Hoyland Ct. Belper DE56 15 C3
Huckerby Rd. Ilk DE7 25 B1
Hufton's Ct. Ship DE75 25 A4
Hufton's Dr. Ship DE75 25 A4
Hulland View. Derby DE22 28 B1
Hunger La. W Und DE6 19 C2
Hunt Ave. Hean DE75 17 C1
Hunter Dr. Kilb DE56 22 C4
Hunter Rd. Belper DE56 15 B3

Ian Ave. Wirk DE4 6 C4
Ilam Sq. Ilk DE7 25 C3
Ilford Cl. Ship DE7 25 B2
Ilkeston Com Hospl. Ilk DE7 25 B2
Ilkeston Rd. Hean DE75 24 C4
Ilkeston Rd. Smal DE7 23 C1
Imperial Ct. Derby DE22 28 B3
Independent Hill. Alf DE55 4 C2
Ingle's Channel. Belper DE56 14 C2
Inglewood Ave. Derby DE3 29 B2
Inn La. Quar DE22 28 A4
Inns La. S Wing DE55 3 C2
Institute La. Alf DE55 5 A2
Intakes La. H Ward DE6 19 B4
Ironville & Codnor Park Prim Sch. Iron NG16 11 C2
Isleworth Dr. Derby DE22 29 C3
Iveagh Wlk. Som DE55 11 C3
Ivy Ct. Derby DE3 29 B1
Ivy Gr. Ripley DE5 10 B1
Ivy La. East NG16 18 C1

Jackass La. Alder DE56 8 A2
Jacksdale Cl. Derby DE22 28 B1
Jackson Ave. Ilk DE7 25 C1
Jackson's La. Heage DE56 15 B4
Jackson's La. Pent DE5 10 A4
Jackson's La. S Wing DE55 4 A1
Jacksons La. Belper DE56 21 C4
James St. Som DE55 11 B4
Jarvey's La. Mack DE22 29 C4
Jasmine Cl. Swan DE55 10 C4
Jebb's La. Idri DE56 12 C4
Jebb's La. Shot DE56 13 A4
Jeffries Ave. Crich DE4 2 C1
Jeffries La. Crich DE4 2 C1
Jenny's Ct. Belper DE56 15 B3
Jervis Ct. Ilk DE7 25 C2
Jesses La. Belper DE56 14 B4

Jessop Ave. Iron NG16 .... 11 C2
Jessop St. Codnor DE5 ...... 17 A4
Jessop St. Ripley DE5 .... 17 A4
Joan Ave. Hean DE75 .... 17 C1
Jodrell Ave. Belper DE56 .... 15 B2
John Flamsteed Com Sch. Denby ...
DE5 .... 16 A1
John O'Gaunts Way. Belper ....
DE56 .... 15 B2
John St. Alf DE55 .... 5 A2
John St. Hean DE75 .... 17 B1
John St. Ilk DE7 .... 25 C1
John St. Som DE55 .... 11 B4
Johnson Dr. Hean DE75 .... 17 C1
Johnson La. Idri DE56 .... 12 C4
Joseph St. Belper DE56 .... 14 C2
Jubilee Ave. Ripley DE5 .... 10 B1
Jubilee Ct. Belper DE56 .... 15 A1
Jubilee Ct. Wirk DE4 .... 6 C4
Julie Ave. Hean DE75 .... 18 A1
Jura Ave. Ripley DE5 .... 10 B1

Kedleston Cl. Derby DE22 ...... 28 B1
Kedleston Cl. Ripley DE5 .... 10 B2
Kedleston Dr. Ilk DE7 .... 25 B2
Kedleston Hall. Mack DE22 ...... 27 C3
Kedleston Rd. Derby DE22 .... 28 A3
Kedleston Rd. Quar DE22 ...... 28 A3
Kedleston Rd. W Und DE22 ... 27 C4
Kendray Cl. Belper DE56 .... 15 B3
Kenilworth Rd. Ripley DE5 ..... 10 B1
Kensington Ave. Hean DE75 .. 17 B1
Keppel Ct. Ilk DE7 .... 25 C2
Kepple Gate. Ripley DE5 .... 16 C4
Kerry Dr. Smal DE7 .... 23 C3
Kerry's Yd. Kilb DE56 .... 22 C4
Kestrel Hts. Iron NG16 .... 11 C2
Kew Cres. Hean DE75 .... 18 A1
Keys Rd. Som DE55 .... 5 A1
Kilbourne Rd. Belper DE56 ..... 15 B2
Kilburn Inf & Jun Schs. Kilb ....
DE56 .... 22 C4
Kilburn La. Denby DE56 .... 15 C2
Kilburn Toll Bar. Kilb DE56 ..... 15 C1
Killis La. Belper DE56 .... 15 B1
Killis La. Holbr DE56 .... 22 B4
Kiln Cl. We Ha DE7 .... 24 C1
Kinder Cres. Bullbr DE56 .... 9 A3
King Edward St. Wirk DE4 .... 7 A4
King George St. Wess DE55 .... 3 C4
King George St. Wirk DE4 .... 6 C4
King St. Alf DE55 .... 4 C2
King St. Belper DE56 .... 14 C2
King St. Duff DE56 .... 21 C2
King St. East NG16 .... 18 C1
King St. Ilk DE7 .... 25 C1
King St. S Norm DE55 .... 5 C3
King William Ctr. Iron NG16 ... 11 C2
King William St. Iron NG16 ... 11 C2
Kings Cl. Hean DE75 .... 17 B1
Kings Croft. Derby DE22 .... 28 C2
Kings Dr. Brin NG16 .... 18 C4
Kingsfield Ind Est. Wirk DE4 ... 6 C3
Kingsfield Rd. Wirk DE4 .... 6 C4
Kingsley Rd. Derby DE22 ...... 28 B2
Kingsmuir Rd. Derby DE3 ...... 29 B2
Kingsway. Hean DE75 .... 17 B1
Kingsway Cres. Kilb DE56 ..... 23 A4
Kingswood Ave. Belper DE56 . 15 B3
Kipling Dr. Derby DE3 .... 29 B1
Kirk Cl. Ripley DE5 .... 16 B4
Kirk Ireton CE Prim Sch. K Ire ....
DE6 .... 6 A1
Kirk Langley CE Prim Sch. K Lang ..
DE6 .... 26 C1
Kirk's La. Belper DE56 .... 15 A2
Kirkham Cl. Hean DE75 .... 17 B1
Kirkham La. Crich DE56 .... 9 A4
Kirkman Rd. Hean DE75 .... 17 B2
Knabhall La. Tans DE4 .... 1 B3
Knapp Ave. East NG16 .... 18 C1
Knob La. Spout DE56 .... 7 B3
Knoll The. Tans DE4 .... 1 A3

Knowl Ave. Belper DE56 .... 14 C3

Laburnum Cres. Derby DE22 . 28 B2
Laburnum Cres. Swan DE55 .. 11 A4
Lacey Cl. Ilk DE7 .... 25 B2
Lacey Fields Rd. Hean DE75 . 18 A1
Ladbroke Gdns. Derby DE22 .. 29 C3
Lady Lea Rd. Hors DE21 .... 23 A3
Lady Ley Hill. Hors DE21 .... 23 A3
Ladybank Rd. Derby DE3 ...... 29 B1
Ladycroft Paddock. Derby ....
DE22 .... 28 C2
Ladyflatts Rd. Wirk DE4 .... 6 C4
Ladywell Ct. Belper DE56 ...... 15 A2
Ladywood Ave. Belper DE56 .. 15 A3
Lake Ave. Hean DE75 .... 17 B2
Lamb Cres. Ripley DE5 .... 10 C1
Lambhouse La. Shot DE56 ..... 13 C3
Lambley Dr. Derby DE22 .... 28 B1
Lambrook Cl. Derby DE3 .... 29 B1
Lambton Cl. Ilk DE7 .... 25 C2
Lander La. Belper DE56 .... 15 A2
Landmere Cl. Ship DE7 .... 25 B2
Laneward Cl. Ilk DE7 .... 25 B2
Langford Rd. Derby DE3 .... 29 B2
Langley Ave. Ilk DE7 .... 25 B3
Langley Ave. Som DE55 .... 11 B4
Langley Inf Sch. Hean DE75 .. 18 A1
Langley Mill CE Inf Sch. La Mill ......
NG16 .... 18 A2
Langley Mill Jun Sch. Ald ....
NG16 .... 18 A2
Langley Mill Sta. Hean NG16 18 A2
Langley Pk. La Mill NG16 ...... 18 A2
Lanscombe Park Rd. Derby ....
DE22 .... 28 C1
Lant La. Ash DE4 .... 1 A4
Larch Ave. Ripley DE5 .... 10 B1
Larch Cl. Derby DE22 .... 28 B2
Larch Cres. East NG16 .... 18 C1
Larch Rd. Kilb DE56 .... 23 A4
Larkhill. Swan DE55 .... 10 C4
Larkhill Cl. Swan DE55 .... 10 C4
Lathkil Dr. S Norm DE55 .... 5 C3
Lathkill Ave. Ilk DE7 .... 25 C3
Lathkill Dr. Ripley DE5 .... 16 B3
Latrigg Cl. Derby DE3 .... 29 C1
Laund Ave. Belper DE56 .... 15 A3
Laund Cl. Belper DE56 .... 15 A3
Laund Hill. Belper DE56 .... 15 A3
Laund Nook. Belper DE56 ...... 15 A3
Laurel Ave. Ripley DE5 .... 10 B1
Laurel Cl. Swan DE55 .... 11 A4
Laurel Cres. Smal DE7 .... 23 C3
Lavender Rd. Swan DE55 ...... 11 A4
Lavender Row. Derby DE22 ... 28 C1
Lawn Ave. Derby DE65 .... 28 B1
Lawn Cl. Hean DE75 .... 17 C1
Lawn Prim Sch. Derby DE22 .. 28 B1
Lawrence Ave. East NG16 ..... 18 C1
Lawrence Ave. Ripley DE5 ..... 16 B4
Lawrence Dr. Brin NG16 .... 18 B4
Lea Cl. Derby DE22 .... 28 C2
Lea Cres. Som DE55 .... 11 B3
Lea Dr. Derby DE3 .... 29 C2
Lea Main Rd. Hollow DE4 .... 2 A4
Lea Moor Rd. Hollow DE4 .... 2 C4
Lea Prim Sch. Hollow DE4 .... 2 A4
Lea Rd. Hollow DE4 .... 2 A4
Lea Wood Croft. Hollow DE4 .... 2 A3
Leabrooks Rd. Som DE55 ...... 11 B4
Leadale Ave. Swan DE55 ...... 11 A4
Leafy La. Hean DE75 .... 17 C1
Leamington St. Ripley DE5 .... 10 C1
Leamoor Ave. Som DE55 .... 11 A4
Leashaw. Crich DE4 .... 2 B2
Leashaw. Hollow DE4 .... 2 B2
Leashaw Rd. Crich DE4 .... 2 B2
Leashaw Rd. Hollow DE4 .... 2 B2
Leche Cft. Belper DE56 .... 15 B2
Ledo Ave. Ripley DE5 .... 10 B1
Lee La. Hean DE75 .... 18 A1
Lees La. S Norm DE55 .... 5 C3

Leniscar Ave. Hean DE75 .... 17 B2
Lens Rd. Derby DE22 .... 28 B1
Leonard Cheshire Cl. Hean ....
DE75 .... 18 A1
Lewcote La. We Ha DE7 .... 25 A1
Ley Ave. Alf DE55 .... 5 A2
Ley Gdns. Alf DE55 .... 5 A2
Leycote Way. Belper DE56 .... 15 A3
Leys Ct. Belper DE56 .... 15 B2
Leys Jun Sch. Alf DE55 .... 5 B2
Leys The. Lit Ea DE21 .... 22 B1
Lickpenny La. Ash DE4 .... 1 C2
Lidgate Cl. Derby DE3 .... 29 B1
Lilac Gr. Hean DE75 .... 17 C1
Lilac Mews. Ilk DE7 .... 25 B2
Lilac Way. Derby DE22 .... 28 B1
Lime Ave. Duff DE56 .... 21 C3
Lime Ave. La Mill NG16 .... 18 B1
Lime Ave. Ripley DE5 .... 10 B1
Lime Cres. Belper DE56 .... 15 A1
Lime Kiln La. Turn DE56 .... 20 A4
Limes Ave. Derby DE3 .... 29 B1
Limes Pk. Ripley DE5 .... 10 B1
Limes The. Mapp DE7 .... 24 C2
Linbery Cl. S Wing DE55 .... 4 A2
Lincoln St. Alf DE55 .... 4 C2
Linden Cl. Kilb DE56 .... 23 A4
Lindrick Cl. Derby DE3 .... 29 C1
Lingfield Rise. Derby DE3 ...... 29 B2
Linkmel Rd. East NG16 .... 18 B2
Linwood Cres. East NG16 ...... 18 C1
Liskeard Dr. Derby DE22 .... 28 B2
Litchen Cl. Ilk DE7 .... 25 C1
Little London. Hollow DE4 .... 2 A3
Little Longstone Cl. Derby DE3 ......
.... 29 C1
Litton Cl. Belper DE56 .... 15 A3
Litton Cl. Ilk DE7 .... 25 C2
Lockton Ave. Hean DE75 .... 24 C4
Lockwood Rd. Derby DE22 .... 28 B2
Lodge Cl. Duff DE56 .... 21 C2
Lodge Dr. Belper DE56 .... 14 C3
Lodge La. Ald NG16 .... 17 C4
Lodge La. Mack DE6, DE22 ... 27 B3
Lodge La. Shot DE56 .... 13 B4
Lodge Rd. Mapp DE7 .... 24 C2
Lodge Way. Derby DE3 .... 29 B1
Lombard St. Derby DE22 .... 29 C3
Long La. K Lang DE6 .... 26 A1
Long La. Lees DE6 .... 26 A1
Long La. Ship DE75 .... 25 B3
Long Meadow Rd. Alf DE55 .... 4 C2
Long Row. Belper DE56 .... 14 C2
Long Row Prim Sch. Belper ....
DE56 .... 14 C3
Longbridge La. Hean DE75 .... 17 B2
Longford Cl. Derby DE22 .... 28 B1
Longstone Rise. Belper DE56 15 A3
Longwalls La. Belper DE56 .... 14 B3
Lons Inf Sch. Ripley DE5 .... 10 B1
Lord Haddon Rd. Ilk DE7 .... 25 C1
Loscoe CE Prim Sch. Hean ....
DE75 .... 17 B2
Loscoe Grange. Hean DE75 ... 17 B2
Loscoe Rd. Hean DE75 .... 17 B1
Loscoe-denby La. Hean ....
DE5, DE75 .... 17 A2
Low Cl. W Und DE6 .... 20 A1
Lower Bloomsgrove Rd. Ilk ....
DE7 .... 25 C1
Lower Chapel St. Ilk DE7 .... 25 C1
Lower Clara Mount Rd. Hean ....
DE75 .... 18 A1
Lower Dr. Swan DE55 .... 10 B4
Lower Dunstead Rd. Ald NG16 18 A2
Lower Dunstead Rd. La Mill ....
NG16 .... 18 A2
Lower Gladstone St. Hean ....
DE75 .... 17 C1
Lower Granby St. Ilk DE7 .... 25 C1
Lower Hall Cl. Holbr DE56 ...... 22 B3
Lower Maples. Hean DE75 ..... 25 A4
Lower Nelson St. Hean DE75 . 17 B1
Lower Rd. Mack DE22 .... 29 C4

Lower Somercotes. Som DE5511 C4
Lowes Hill. Ripley DE5 .... 10 B2
Lowlands Lea. Hean DE75 ..... 17 C1
Lowlands Rd. Belper DE56 .... 15 A2
Loxton Ct. Derby DE3 .... 29 B2
Ludgate Wlk. Derby DE22 ...... 29 C3
Lumb La. Haz DE56 .... 14 A2
Lumber La. H Ward DE6 .... 12 B1
Lydford Rd. Alf DE55 .... 5 A3
Lydia Gdns. East NG16 .... 18 C1
Lynam Rd. Fritch DE56 .... 9 B4
Lynam Rd. S Wing DE56 .... 9 B4
Lyncroft Ave. Ripley DE5 .... 10 C1
Lyndale Dr. Codnor DE5 .... 17 A4
Lynmouth Dr. Ship DE7 .... 25 B2
Lynton Cl. Ripley DE5 .... 10 B2
Lynton Rd. Amber DE56 .... 9 A2

Madeley Ct. Derby DE3 .... 29 B1
Mag La. Idri DE56 .... 12 B3
Magnolia Way. Swan DE55 .... 11 A4
Maidwell Cl. Belper DE56 ...... 15 B3
Main Ave. Derby DE22 .... 28 C3
Main Rd. Crich DE4 .... 2 B1
Main Rd. Pent DE5 .... 10 B3
Main Rd. Ripley DE5 .... 10 A2
Main Rd. Smal DE7 .... 23 C2
Main Rd. Som DE55 .... 11 C3
Main St. East NG16 .... 18 C1
Main St. H Wood DE7 .... 23 B3
Main St. K Ire DE6 .... 6 A1
Main St. Mapp DE7 .... 24 C2
Mais Cl. Tans DE4 .... 1 A3
Makeney Rd. Belper DE56 ..... 22 A3
Makeney Rd. Duff DE56 .... 21 C1
Makeney Rd. Holbr DE56 ...... 22 B3
Malinscommon La. Spout DE56 .....
.... 7 B2
Maltby Cl. Derby DE22 .... 28 C1
Malthouse Cl. East NG16 ...... 18 C1
Malthouse La. N Heage DE56 .. 9 A1
Malvern Cl. Derby DE3 .... 29 B2
Manners Ave. Ilk DE7 .... 25 B1
Manners Ind Est. Ilk DE7 .... 25 C1
Manners Rd. Ilk DE7 .... 25 C1
Manning View. Ilk DE7 .... 25 C1
Manor Croft. Ripley DE5 .... 10 B2
Manor Ct. Som DE55 .... 11 C3
Manor Rd. Belper DE56 .... 14 C2
Manor Rd. East NG16 .... 18 C1
Manor Rd. Ilk DE7 .... 25 C1
Manor Rd. S Wing DE55 .... 3 C2
Mansfield Rd. Alf DE55 .... 5 A2
Mansfield Rd. Brin NG16 .... 18 C2
Mansfield Rd. East NG16 .... 18 C2
Mansfield Rd. Hean DE75 ...... 18 A1
Mansfield St. Som DE55 .... 11 B4
Manvers Ave. Ripley DE5 ...... 10 C1
Manvers St. Ripley DE5 .... 10 C1
Maple Ave. Ripley DE5 .... 16 B4
Maple Dr. Belper DE56 .... 15 A1
Maple Gdns. Hean DE75 .... 17 B1
Maple Gr. Derby DE72 .... 28 B3
Mapperley CE Prim Sch. Mapp ......
DE7 .... 24 C2
Mapperley La. Mapp DE7 ...... 24 C1
Marchington Cl. Derby DE22 . 28 C1
Marfleet Cl. Derby DE3 .... 29 B2
Marina Rd. Smal DE7 .... 24 A4
Market Pl. Belper DE56 .... 15 A2
Market Pl. Codnor DE5 .... 17 A4
Market Pl. Crich DE4 .... 2 C1
Market Pl. Iron NG16 .... 11 C2
Market Pl. Ridd DE55 .... 11 C3
Market Pl. Ripley DE5 .... 10 B1
Market Pl. Som DE55 .... 11 B4
Market Pl. Wirk DE4 .... 6 C4
Market St. Hean DE75 .... 17 C1
Market St. Iron NG16 .... 11 C2
Marlborough Dr. Belper DE56 15 B3
Marlpool Inf Sch. Hean DE75 . 25 A4
Marlpool Jun Sch. Hean DE75 18 A1
Marsden Cl. Duff DE56 .... 21 C2

Marsh La. Belper DE56 .... 15 A3
Marsh Lane Cres. Belper DE56 ....
.... 15 A2
Marshall St. Alf DE55 .... 5 A2
Marshall St. Hean DE75 .... 17 C1
Marshaw Cl. Derby DE3 .... 29 C1
Marston Cl. Belper DE56 .... 15 B3
Martindale Ct. Belper DE56 .... 15 B3
Mary Howitt Inf Com Sch. Hean
DE75 .... 17 B1
Mason Rd. Ilk DE7 .... 25 B1
Matlock Rd. Amber DE56 .... 8 C2
Matlock Rd. Belper DE56 ...... 14 C4
Matlock Rd. Wess DE55 .... 3 C4
May South. Ilk DE7 .... 25 B2
May St. Ilk DE7 .... 25 C2
Mayfair Cres. Derby DE22 ..... 29 C3
Mayfield Ave. Hean DE75 ...... 17 C1
Mayfield Ave. Kilb DE56 .... 23 A4
Meadow Ave. Codnor DE5 ...... 17 A4
Meadow Cl. East NG16 .... 18 C2
Meadow Cl. H Wood DE7 .... 23 B3
Meadow Ct. Belper DE56 .... 14 C2
Meadow Ct. Kilb DE56 .... 23 A4
Meadow Ct. S Norm DE55 .... 5 C2
Meadow La. Newt DE55 .... 5 C4
Meadow Lane Ind Est. Alf DE55 .....
.... 5 A3
Meadow Rd. Ripley DE5 .... 10 C1
Meadow St. Ilk DE7 .... 25 C1
Meadow St. Iron NG16 .... 11 C3
Meadow Vale. Duff DE56 .... 21 B2
Meadow View. S Wing DE55 ... 3 C3
Meadowbank Way. East NG16 18 B2
Meadows Croft. Duff DE56 .... 21 B2
Meadows Prim Sch The. Duff ....
DE56 .... 21 B2
Meadows The. Hean DE75 ..... 17 C1
Meadows The. Swan DE55 ..... 10 C4
Melbourn Cl. Duff DE56 .... 21 C2
Melbourne Cl. Belper DE56 .... 15 A1
Melbourne Cl. Derby DE3 ...... 28 B1
Melbourne Cl. Derby DE3 ...... 29 C2
Melbreak Cl. Derby DE3 .... 29 C1
Mellor's La. Holbr DE56 .... 22 B3
Melton Ct. Som DE55 .... 11 B3
Memorial Rd. Derby DE22 ..... 28 B2
Menin Rd. Derby DE22 .... 28 B1
Mentmore Cl. Swan DE55 ...... 11 A4
Mercaston La. H Ward DE6 .... 19 A2
Mercaston La. Mack ....
DE6, DE22 .... 27 A4
Mercaston La. W Und ....
DE6, DE22 .... 27 A4
Mercer Cres. Alf DE55 .... 5 B2
Meridian Cl. Ilk DE7 .... 25 C2
Merlin Cl. Belper DE56 .... 15 B3
Meynell Ct. Derby DE22 .... 28 B1
Michael House-Rudolf Steiner Sch.
Ship DE75 .... 25 A3
Micklebring Cl. Ripley DE5 .... 10 B1
Mickleover Prim Sch. Derby ....
DE3 .... 29 B1
Mickleross Cl. Derby DE3 ...... 29 B2
Middleton Ave. Codnor DE5 ... 17 A3
Middle La. Crich DE4 .... 2 B1
Midland Railway Ctr. Ripley ....
DE5 .... 10 C2
Midland Rd. East NG16 .... 18 C1
Midland Rd. Hean DE75 .... 17 C1
Midland Terr. Amber DE56 ...... 8 C2
Midway. Derby DE22 .... 28 C1
Milbank Cl. Derby DE3 .... 29 C3
Mile Ash La. Derby DE22 ...... 28 C1
Milford Dr. Ilk DE7 .... 25 B2
Milford Prim Sch. Belper DE56 .....
.... 21 C4
Milford Rd. Duff DE56 .... 21 C2
Millbank Ave. Belper DE56 .... 15 A1
Mill Cl. Kilb DE56 .... 23 A4
Mill Cl. Swan DE55 .... 10 C4
Mill Croft. Derby DE22 .... 29 B2
Mill Hil Sch. Ripley DE5 .... 16 C4
Mill La. Belper DE56 .... 15 A2

Mill La. Codnor DE5 .... 17 A4
Mill La. Derby DE74 .... 29 B2
Mill La. Hollow DE4 .... 2 A3
Mill Rd. Hean DE75 .... 25 A4
Mill St. Belper DE56 .... 15 A2
Mill St. Ilk DE7 .... 25 C1
Mill Yd. Som DE55 .... 11 B4
Millbank. Hean DE75 .... 24 A4
Millbank Cl. Ship DE7 .... 25 B2
Milldale Cl. Ripley DE5 .... 16 B3
Milldale Ct. Belper DE56 .... 15 A2
Millers Dale Cl. Belper DE56 . 15 B3
Millers Gn. Wirk DE4 .... 6 C3
Millersdale Ave. Ilk DE7 .... 25 C3
Millfield Cl. Ilk DE7 .... 25 B2
Mills Ct. Crich DE4 .... 2 C1
Millstone La. Pent DE5 .... 10 B4
Milner Ave. Codnor DE5 .... 17 A4
Milnhay Rd. Hean NG16 .... 18 B1
Milnhay Rd. La Mill NG16 ...... 18 B1
Milton Ave. Alf DE55 .... 5 B2
Milton Ave. Ilk DE7 .... 25 C2
Milton Rd. Derby DE65 .... 29 B2
Milton Rd. Ilk DE7 .... 25 C2
Milton St. Ilk DE7 .... 25 C2
Milward Rd. Hean DE75 .... 17 B1
Minster Way. Swan DE55 ...... 10 C4
Misterton Cl. Derby DE22 ...... 28 C1
Mitchell Ave. La Mill NG16 .... 18 A2
Monk Rd. Som DE55 .... 5 A1
Monkton Cl. Ship DE7 .... 25 B2
Monsal Dr. S Norm DE55 .... 5 C3
Monsall Ave. Ilk DE7 .... 25 C3
Montpelier. Quar DE22 .... 28 B4
Montpelier Rd. Amber DE56 .... 8 C2
Monument Hill. Iron NG16 .... 11 C2
Monument La. Iron NG16 ...... 11 C2
Monyash Cl. Ilk DE7 .... 25 C2
Monyash Way. Belper DE56 ... 15 A3
Moor La. Callow DE4 .... 6 A2
Moor La. K Ire DE6 .... 6 A2
Moor La. K Lang DE6 .... 26 C1
Moor La. Lit Ea DE21 .... 22 C1
Moor Rd. Brin NG16 .... 18 C4
Moor Rise. Holbr DE56 .... 22 B4
Moor The. Brin NG16 .... 18 B4
Mooredge Rd. Crich DE4 .... 3 A1
Moorfield Rd. Holbr DE56 ...... 22 B4
Moorfields Ave. East NG16 .... 18 C2
Moorgate. Derby DE22 .... 29 C3
Moorland Rd. Derby DE3 .... 29 B2
Moorpool Cres. Holbr DE56 ... 22 B4
Moorside La. Holbr DE56 ...... 22 B4
Moorwoodmoor La. Wess DE55
.... 3 B3
Morley Cl. Belper DE56 .... 15 C3
Morley Dr. Ilk DE7 .... 25 B2
Morleyfields Cl. Ripley DE5 ... 10 C1
Morrell Wood Dr. Belper DE56 15 B3
Mortimer Wilson Sch. Alf DE55 5 A2
Moseley St. Ripley DE5 .... 10 B1
Moss La. Ripley DE5 .... 10 B2
Moulton Cl. Belper DE56 .... 15 B3
Moulton Cl. Swan DE55 .... 10 C4
Mount Pleasant. Ilk DE7 .... 25 C2
Mount Pleasant. Ripley DE5 ... 10 B1
Mount Pleasant. Som DE55 ... 11 B3
Mount Pleasant Dr. Belper ....
DE56 .... 14 C3
Mount Pleasant Dr. Heage ....
DE56 .... 15 C4
Mount St. Hean DE75 .... 17 C1
Mountbatten Ct. Ilk DE7 .... 25 C2
Mountford Ave. Wirk DE4 .... 6 C4
Muggington CE Prim Sch. ....
W Und DE6 .... 19 C1
Muirfield Dr. Derby DE3 .... 29 C1
Mulberry Cl. Belper DE56 ...... 15 A2
Mulberry Mews. Ripley DE5 ... 16 B3
Mullberries Ct. Derby DE22 ... 28 C2
Mundy CE Jun Sch. Hean ....
DE75 .... 17 C1
Mundy St. Hean DE75 .... 17 C1
Mundy St. Ilk DE7 .... 25 C1

Mundy's Dr. Hean DE75 .... 24 C4
Murray Park Com Sch. Derby ....
DE3 .... 29 C2
Murray Rd. Derby DE3 .... 29 C2
Muskham Ave. Ilk DE7 .... 25 C2
Muswell Rd. Derby DE22 .... 29 C3

Nailers Way. Belper DE56 ...... 15 B3
Napier Cl. Derby DE3 .... 29 C2
Naseby Cl. Derby DE3 .... 29 B2
Naseby Rd. Belper DE56 .... 15 B2
National Tramway Mus. Crich ......
DE4 .... 2 C1
Neal Ct. La Mill NG16 .... 18 A2
Needham St. Codnor DE5 ...... 17 A4
Nelson Cl. Derby DE3 .... 29 C2
Nelson St. Ilk DE7 .... 25 C2
Nesfield Cl. Ilk DE7 .... 25 C1
Nesfield Rd. Ilk DE7 .... 25 C1
Ness Wlk. Derby DE22 .... 28 C2
Nether Cl. Duff DE56 .... 21 C3
Nether Cl. East NG16 .... 18 C2
Nether Cl. Swan DE55 .... 10 C4
Nether Gdns. Wirk DE4 .... 6 C4
Nether La. Haz DE56 .... 21 A4
Nether La. Holbr DE56 .... 22 B3
Nether La. K Ire DE56 .... 12 A4
Netherwood Ct. Derby DE22 .. 28 B2
New Breck Rd. Belper DE56 ... 15 A2
New Derby Rd. East NG16 ..... 18 B1
New Rd. Belper DE56 .... 14 C2
New Rd. Crich DE4 .... 9 A4
New Rd. Heage DE56 .... 15 B4
New Rd. Idri DE56 .... 12 C3
New Rd. Iron NG16 .... 11 C2
New Rd. Ridge DE56 .... 9 A2
New Rd. Som DE5, NG16 .... 11 B1
New Rd. W Und DE6 .... 19 B1
New St. Alf DE55 .... 5 A2
New St. Ripley DE5 .... 10 C1
New St. Som DE55 .... 11 B4
New St. Swan DE55 .... 10 C4
New Zealand La. Duff DE56 ... 21 C1
Newbridge Rd. N Heage DE56 . 9 A1
Newham Ave. Ripley DE5 ...... 10 B1
Newham Cl. Hean DE75 .... 18 A1
Newlands Dr. Hean DE75 ...... 17 C2
Newlands Dr. Som DE55 .... 11 B3
Newlands Rd. Som DE55 .... 11 B3
Newmanleys Rd. East NG16 .. 25 C4
Newmanleys Rd S. East NG16 25 C4
Newstead Rd S. Ilk DE7 .... 25 B2
Newton Cl. Belper DE56 .... 15 B3
Nightingale Cl. Ripley DE5 .... 10 B1
Nodin Hill La. N Heage DE56 .. 9 A2
Nook End Rd. Hean DE75 ...... 17 B1
Nook The. Hean DE75 .... 17 B2
Nook The. Holbr DE56 .... 22 B4
Norbury Cl. Derby DE22 .... 28 C1
Norbury Ct. Derby DE22 .... 28 B1
Norbury Way. Belper DE56 .... 15 B3
Norman Cres. Ilk DE7 .... 25 C2
Norman Rd. Ripley DE5 .... 10 B1
Norman Rd. Som DE55 .... 11 C4
Norman St. Ilk DE7 .... 25 C2
Normanton Ave. Alf DE55 .... 5 B2
North Ave. Derby DE3 .... 29 C1
North Cl. Derby DE65 .... 29 C2
North Cl. S Norm DE55 .... 5 C3
North La. Belper DE56 .... 14 B1
North La. Belper DE56 .... 21 C4
North St. Alf DE55 .... 5 A2
North St. La Mill NG16 .... 18 A2
North St. Som DE55 .... 11 B3
North St. S Norm DE55 .... 5 B2
North St. Ilk DE7 .... 25 C1
North View. Crich DE4 .... 9 A4
Northam Dr. Ripley DE5 .... 10 B2
Northern Rd. Hean DE75 .... 17 B1
Northfield. Kilb DE56 .... 15 C1
Northfield Ave. Ilk DE7 .... 25 C1
Northgate St. Ilk DE7 .... 25 C1
Nottingham La. Iron NG16 .... 11 C3

Nottingham La. Som ....
DE55, NG16 .... 11 C3
Nottingham Rd. Alf DE55 .... 5 A1
Nottingham Rd. Belper DE56 . 15 A2
Nottingham Rd. Codnor DE5 .. 17 B4
Nottingham Rd. East NG16 .... 18 C1
Nottingham Rd. Ripley DE5 ... 10 C1
Nottingham Rd. Som DE55 ...... 5 A1
Nottingham Rd. Tans DE4 .... 1 A2
Nursery Croft. Wirk DE4 .... 6 C3
Nuttall Cl. Alf DE55 .... 4 C2
Nuttall St. Alf DE55 .... 4 C2

Oak Ave. Ald NG16 .... 18 A3
Oak Ave. Ripley DE5 .... 16 B4
Oak Cl. Derby DE72 .... 28 C2
Oak Cl. Duff DE56 .... 21 C1
Oak Dr. Alf DE55 .... 5 A2
Oak Dr. Derby DE65 .... 29 C1
Oak Dr. East NG16 .... 18 C1
Oak Tree Gdns. Tans DE4 .... 1 A2
Oakes's Row. Iron NG16 .... 11 C3
Oakfield Ct. Stanl DE7 .... 24 A1
Oakham Way. Ilk DE7 .... 25 C2
Oakhurst Cl. Belper DE56 ...... 14 B3
Oakland Cres. Som DE55 ...... 11 B3
Oakland St. Alf DE55 .... 5 A2
Oaklands Ave. Hean DE75 ..... 18 A1
Oaklands Cl. Denby DE56 ...... 16 B1
Oakover Dr. Derby DE22 .... 28 B1
Oaksedge La. Tans DE4 .... 1 A3
Oaktree Cl. Swan DE55 .... 11 A4
Oat Hill. Wirk DE4 .... 6 C4
Ochbrook Ct. Ilk DE7 .... 25 C2
Old Church La. Quar DE22 .... 28 B3
Old Coppice Side. Hean DE75 24 C4
Old Derby Rd. East NG16 ...... 18 B2
Old Hall Ave. Duff DE56 .... 21 C2
Old Hartshay Hill. Ripley DE5 10 B1
Old Highcliff La. Turn DE56 ... 13 A2
Old La. Idri DE56 .... 13 A3
Old Mill Cl. Duff DE56 .... 21 C2
Old Pit La. Smal DE7 .... 24 A3
Old Pond The. Hean DE75 ..... 25 A4
Old Rd. Heage DE56 .... 15 C4
Old Vicarage La. Quar DE22 .. 28 B3
Oliver Cl. Hean DE75 .... 18 A1
Olton Rd. Derby DE3 .... 29 B2
Onslow Rd. Derby DE3 .... 29 C2
Openacre. Iron NG16 .... 11 C2
Openwood Rd. Denby DE56 ... 15 C2
Openwoodgate. Belper DE56 . 15 B2
Orange St. Alf DE55 .... 5 A2
Orchard Bsns Pk. Ilk DE7 ...... 25 B1
Orchard Cl. Belper DE56 .... 22 A4
Orchard Cl. Ripley DE5 .... 17 A4
Orchard Cotts. Duff DE56 ...... 21 C2
Orchard Cres. Swan DE55 ..... 10 B4
Orchard Ct. La Mill NG16 ...... 18 A2
Orchard Rd. Som DE55 .... 11 B3
Orchard Rise. Hean DE75 ..... 17 C1
Orchard St. Derby DE3 .... 29 B1
Orchard St. La Mill NG16 ...... 18 A2
Orchard The. Belper DE56 ..... 15 A2
Orchard The. Codnor DE5 ..... 11 A1
Orchard The. H Wood DE7 ..... 23 B3
Orchards The. Derby DE22 .... 28 B2
Ormonde St. Ald NG16 .... 18 A2
Ormonde Terr. Ald NG16 .... 18 A2
Orton Way. Belper DE56 .... 15 A3
Otterburn Dr. Derby DE22 ..... 28 B1
Outram Ct. Ripley DE5 .... 10 C1
Outram St. Ripley DE5 .... 10 C1
Outseats Dr. Alf DE55 .... 5 A2
Over La. Belper DE56 .... 15 C3
Over La. Haz DE56 .... 14 A1
Overstone Cl. Belper DE56 .... 15 B2
Owers Ave. Hean DE75 .... 24 C4
Owlston Cl. East NG16 .... 18 C2
Oxford St. East NG16 .... 18 C1
Oxford St. Ripley DE5 .... 10 B1

Padley Cl. Ripley DE5 .... 10 B2
Palace La. Shot DE56 .... 7 B1
Palerow La. Alder DE56 .... 7 C2
Palerow La. Spout DE56 .... 7 C2
Palmer Dr. Swan DE55 .... 10 C4
Parade The. Derby DE3 .... 29 B1
Park Ave. East NG16 .... 18 C2
Park Ave. Ripley DE5 .... 10 C1
Park Cl. Kilb DE56 .... 23 A4
Park Cres. East NG16 .... 18 C2
Park Cres. Heage DE56 .... 15 C4
Park Ct. Hean DE75 .... 17 C1
Park Dr. Swan DE55 .... 10 C3
Park Farm Ctr. Derby DE22 .... 28 B1
Park Farm Dr. Derby DE22 ..... 28 B1
Park Hall Rd. Denby DE5 .... 16 A2
Park La. Derby DE22 .... 28 C2
Park La. Pent DE5 .... 10 A4
Park La. Shirl DE55 .... 5 A4
Park La. S Wing DE55 .... 3 B1
Park Mews. Som DE55 .... 11 B3
Park Mill Dr. Black DE55 .... 5 B4
Park Rd. Belper DE56 .... 15 A1
Park Rd. Derby DE3 .... 29 B1
Park Rd. Duff DE56 .... 21 B2
Park Rd. Heage DE56 .... 15 C4
Park Rd. Ripley DE5 .... 10 C1
Park Side. Som DE55 .... 11 B4
Park St. Alf DE55 .... 4 C2
Park St. Hean DE75 .... 17 B1
Park St. Ripley DE5 .... 10 C1
Park St. Wess DE55 .... 3 C4
Park View. Hean DE75 .... 17 B1
Park View. Som DE55 .... 11 B3
Park View Cl. Derby DE3 .... 29 B1
Parkhouse Dr. S Norm DE55 .... 5 C3
Parkin St. Alf DE55 .... 5 A2
Parks Ave. S Wing DE55 .... 3 C2
Parkside. Heage DE56 .... 15 C4
Parkside Cl. Iron NG16 .... 11 C2
Parkside Dr. Iron NG16 .... 11 C2
Parkstone Ct. Derby DE3 .... 29 B1
Parkwood Sch. Alf DE55 .... 4 C2
Parsons Gr. Denby DE5 .... 16 B1
Pasteur Ave. Ripley DE5 .... 10 B1
Pastures The. Duff DE56 .... 21 C2
Pavilion Rd. Ilk DE7 .... 25 C3
Paxton Cl. Derby DE3 .... 29 B1
Peach St. Hean DE75 .... 17 B1
Peacock Pl. Ilk DE7 .... 25 B2
Peacock Way. Swan DE55 ..... 10 C4
Peak Ave. Som DE55 .... 11 A3
Peak View. S Norm DE55 .... 5 C3
Peakdale Cl. Ripley DE5 .... 16 B3
Pear Tree Ave. Ripley DE5 ..... 16 B4
Pease Cl. Alf DE55 .... 5 A2
Pease Hill. Alf DE55 .... 5 A2
Peasehill. Ripley DE5 .... 16 C4
Peasehill Rd. Ripley DE5 .... 16 C4
Peat La. Spout DE56 .... 7 B2
Peatburn Ave. Hean DE75 ...... 17 B1
Peats Cl. K Ire DE6 .... 6 A1
Peel St. La Mill NG16 .... 18 A2
Pelham Ave. Ilk DE7 .... 25 C1
Pendlebury Dr. Derby DE3 ..... 29 C1
Pendleton La. Alder DE56 .... 7 C4
Penine View. Heage DE56 ..... 15 C4
Penn St. Belper DE56 .... 15 A2
Pennine Ave. Som DE55 .... 11 B4
Pennine Dr. S Norm DE55 .... 5 C3
Pennytown Ct. Som DE55 .... 5 B1
Pentewen Cl. Derby DE22 ...... 28 C1
Pentrich Rd. Ripley DE5 .... 10 B1
Pentrich Rd. Swan DE55 .... 10 B4
Perth Cl. Derby DE3 .... 29 C2
Peterway. Som DE55 .... 11 B4
Petty Close La. K Lang DE6 .... 26 B1
Peveril Cl. Som DE55 .... 11 B3
Peveril Ct. Ripley DE5 .... 10 B1
Peveril Dr. Ilk DE7 .... 25 B1
Peveril Dr. Som DE55 .... 11 B3
Philips Croft. Duff DE56 .... 21 C2
Philipway. Som DE55 .... 11 B4
Pickard La. Heage DE56 .... 9 B1

Pickering Ave. East NG16 ...... 18 C1
Pillar Butts. Wirk DE4 .... 6 C4
Pilsley Cl. Belper DE56 .... 15 B3
Pimm's Rd. K Lang DE6 .... 29 A4
Pinchom's Hill Rd. Belper
DE56 .... 15 A2
Pine Ave. La Mill NG16 .... 18 A2
Pine Cl. Ripley DE5 .... 10 B1
Pine Cl. Smal DE7 .... 23 C3
Pine Tree Wlk. East NG16 ...... 18 B1
Pinewood Ave. Codnor DE5 ... 17 A4
Pinewood Rd. Belper DE56 .... 14 C3
Pinfold The. Belper DE56 .... 15 B3
Pingle. Derby DE22 .... 28 C2
Pingle Cres. Belper DE56 ...... 14 C3
Pingle La. Belper DE56 .... 14 C3
Pippin Hill. Denby DE5 .... 16 C1
Pit Farm. Ripley DE55 .... 11 A2
Pit La. Codnor DE5 .... 17 A4
Pit La. Crich DE4 .... 3 A3
Pit La. Ripley DE5 .... 10 C1
Pit La. Ship DE75 .... 25 A3
Pit La. Shirl DE55 .... 4 B4
Pittyway Rd. Wirk DE4 .... 6 C4
Plains La. Haz DE56 .... 14 A2
Plaistow Green Rd. Crich DE4 . 2 C1
Platts Ave. Hean DE75 .... 17 B1
Plough Gate. Derby DE22 ...... 28 C1
Plumptre. Ald NG16 .... 18 A3
Plumptre Cl. East NG16 .... 18 C1
Plumptre Way. East NG16 ...... 18 C1
Pole's Rd. K Lang DE6 .... 29 A4
Pond Rd. Holbr DE56 .... 22 B4
Poplar Ave. Ripley DE5 .... 16 B4
Poplar Nook. Derby DE22 ...... 28 C2
Poplars The. Derby DE22 ...... 28 C2
Port Way. Holbr DE21, DE56 .. 22 B3
Porterhouse Rd. Ripley DE5 .. 10 C1
Portland Cl. Derby DE3 .... 29 B1
Portland Rd. Ilk DE7 .... 25 C2
Portreath Dr. Derby DE22 ...... 28 C2
Portway Inf & Jun Sch. Derby
DE22 .... 28 C2
Potters La. Crich DE4 .... 3 A3
Pottery Cl. Belper DE56 .... 15 B3
Pottery La. Denby DE5 .... 16 B2
Pottery Prim Sch. Belper DE56
.... 15 B2
Poynter Cl. Hean DE75 .... 17 B1
Poyser La. K Lang DE6 .... 27 A1
Pratthall La. Wirk DE56 .... 7 A3
Prescot Cl. Derby DE3 .... 29 B1
Prestom Ave. Alf DE55 .... 5 A2
Preston Ave. Alf DE55 .... 5 A2
Primary Cl. Belper DE56 .... 15 A2
Primrose St. Ilk DE7 .... 25 C2
Prince St. Ilk DE7 .... 25 C2
Princess St. East NG16 .... 18 C2
Priory Gdns. Swan DE55 .... 11 A4
Priory Rd. Alf DE55 .... 5 A3
Priory Rd. East NG16 .... 18 C1
Prospect Ave. S Norm DE55 .... 5 C3
Prospect Dr. Belper DE56 ..... 14 C1
Prospect Rd. Denby DE5 .... 16 A1
Prospect Rd. Hean DE75 .... 25 A4
Prospect St. Alf DE55 .... 5 A2
Prospect Terr. Crich DE4 .... 9 A4
Providence Pl. Alf DE55 .... 4 C2
Providence Pl. Ilk DE7 .... 25 C1
Providence St. Ripley DE5 ..... 16 C4
Purchase Ave. Hean DE75 ..... 17 B1
Putney Cl. Derby DE22 .... 29 C3
Pye Bridge Ind Est. Som DE55 11 C3
Pytchley Cl. Belper DE56 ...... 15 B2

Quarn Dr. Derby DE22 .... 28 B2
Quarndon Hts. Derby DE22 .... 28 B2
Quarndon View. Derby DE22 .. 28 B1
Quarry Rd. Belper DE56 .... 14 C1
Quarry Rd. Morley DE7 .... 23 A1
Quarry Rd. Som DE55 .... 11 B4
Queen St. Belper DE56 .... 15 A2
Queen St. Iron NG16 .... 11 C2

Queen St. La Mill NG16 .... 18 B2
Queen St. Ripley DE5 .... 17 A4
Queen St. Som DE55 .... 11 B4
Queen St. S Norm DE55 .... 5 C3
Queen's Dr. Belper DE56 ...... 14 C3
Queen's Sq. East NG16 .... 18 C1
Queens Ave. Hean DE75 .... 17 B1
Queens Dr. Brin NG16 .... 18 C4
Queens Rd N. East NG16 ...... 18 C1
Queens Rd S. East NG16 ...... 18 C1
Queensland Cl. Derby DE3 ... 29 C2
Queensview Dr. Ripley DE5 ... 17 A4
Queensway. Derby DE22 ...... 28 C1
Quenby La. Ripley DE5 .... 10 C1

Radbourne La. Derby DE22 ... 29 C3
Radford Rd. Smal DE7 .... 23 C3
Raglan St. Alf DE55 .... 5 A2
Railway Row. Iron NG16 .... 11 C2
Raleigh Cl. Ilk DE7 .... 25 C2
Ralph Dr. Som DE55 .... 11 B4
Rangemore Cl. Derby DE3 .... 29 C2
Rannoch Cl. Derby DE22 ...... 28 C2
Ratcliffe St. East NG16 .... 18 C1
Raven Cl. Som DE55 .... 11 B3
Raven Oak Cl. Belper DE56 ... 15 A2
Ravensdale Inf & Jun Sch. Derby
DE3 .... 29 C2
Ravensdale Rd. Derby DE22 .. 28 B2
Rawson Gn. Kilb DE56 .... 15 C1
Ray St. Hean DE75 .... 17 C1
Ray's Ave. Hean DE75 .... 17 C1
Rayneham Rd. Ilk DE7 .... 25 B2
Recreation Rd. Wirk DE4 .... 6 C4
Rectory La. K Ire DE6 .... 6 A1
Red Hill. Tans DE4 .... 1 B2
Red Hill La. Tans DE4 .... 1 B2
Red La. Belper DE56 .... 22 A3
Red La. S Norm DE55 .... 5 C2
Red Lion Sq. Hean DE75 .... 17 C1
Redfern Ave. Ripley DE5 .... 10 C1
Redland Cl. Ilk DE7 .... 25 C2
Redmoor Cl. Codnor DE5 ...... 11 A1
Regent Ct. Iron NG16 .... 11 C2
Regent St. La Mill NG16 .... 18 A2
Reigate Prim Sch. Derby DE22
.... 29 C4
Revill Cl. Ilk DE7 .... 25 B1
Reynolds Ave. Ripley DE5 ..... 10 C1
Ribblesdale Cl. Derby DE22 .. 28 B1
Riber Ave. Som DE55 .... 11 B4
Riber Rd. Hollow DE4 .... 2 A4
Riber View Cl. Tans DE4 .... 1 A3
Richardson Dr. Smal DE7 ...... 23 C3
Richardson Endowed Prim Sch.
Smal DE7 .... 23 C3
Richardsons La. Som DE55 ... 11 B3
Richmond Ave. Ilk DE7 .... 25 C2
Richmond Dr. Duff DE56 .... 21 B3
Riddings. Derby DE22 .... 28 C2
Riddings Inf Sch. Som DE55 . 11 B3
Riddings Jun Sch. Som DE55 11 B3
Ridgedale View. Ripley DE5 .. 10 B1
Ridgeway. Hean DE75 .... 24 C4
Ridgeway La. Ridge DE56 .... 9 B2
Rigga La. Lit Ea DE56 .... 22 A1
Rigley Ave. Ilk DE7 .... 25 C1
Rigsby Ct. Derby DE3 .... 29 B2
Riley Ave. Wess DE55 .... 3 C4
Riley La. Pent DE5 .... 10 A3
Ripley Hospl. Ripley DE5 ...... 10 B1
Ripley Inf Sch. Ripley DE5 .... 16 B4
Ripley Jun Sch. Ripley DE5 ... 16 B4
Ripley Rd. Bullbr DE56 .... 9 B3
Rise The. Derby DE22 .... 28 C1
Risley Ct. Ilk DE7 .... 25 C2
River Gdns. Belper DE56 ...... 14 C3
River View. Belper DE56 .... 21 C4
Riversdale. Ridge DE56 .... 9 A2
Roberts Dr. Alf DE55 .... 5 A2
Robey Dr. East NG16 .... 18 C2
Robin Croft Rd. Derby DE22 .. 28 C2
Robin Hood Cl. East NG16 .... 18 C1

Rockeries The. Heage DE56 .... 9 C1
Rocks The. Tans DE4 .... 1 A3
Rodger's La. Alf DE55 .... 5 A3
Rodney Way. Ilk DE7 .... 25 C2
Roe's La. Crich DE4 .... 3 A1
Romsley Cl. Derby DE3 .... 29 B2
Rood La. Idri DE56 .... 12 C3
Roper Ave. Hean DE75 .... 24 C4
Ropewalk The. Hean DE75 .... 24 C4
Ropewalk The. Stanl DE7 ...... 24 A1
Rose Ave. Ilk DE7 .... 25 C1
Rosemount Ct. Derby DE22 .. 28 B2
Rosewood Cres. Hean DE75 .. 18 A1
Rosier Cres. Swan DE55 .... 11 A4
Rossendale. Ilk DE7 .... 25 C2
Rothwell La. Belper DE56 ...... 15 A2
Rothwell Rd. Derby DE3 .... 29 B2
Roughpiece La. Spout DE56 ... 7 B3
Rowan Ave. Ripley DE5 .... 16 B4
Rowan Dr. Kilb DE56 .... 23 A4
Rowland Ct. Alf DE55 .... 4 C2
Rowland St. Alf DE55 .... 5 A2
Rowthorne Ave. Swan DE55 .. 11 A4
Royal Gate. Belper DE56 ...... 15 B2
Roydon Cl. Derby DE3 .... 29 B2
Royston Dr. Belper DE56 ...... 15 B3
Ruffstone Cl. Holbr DE56 ...... 22 B4
Rugby Ave. Alf DE55 .... 5 B2
Rutland Ave. Ripley DE5 .... 17 A4
Rutland Ct. Ilk DE7 .... 25 B1
Rutland Dr. Derby DE3 .... 29 C2
Rutland Pl. Bullbr DE56 .... 9 A3
Rutland St. Ilk DE7 .... 25 C1
Rutland Terr. Ilk DE7 .... 25 C1
Rydal Cl. Ilk DE7 .... 25 C2
Ryegrass Cl. Belper DE56 ..... 15 B2
Ryemere Cl. East NG16 .... 18 C1
Ryknield Hill. Denby DE5 ...... 16 A1
Ryknield Rd. Kilb DE56 .... 23 A4

Salcey Cl. Swan DE55 .... 10 C4
Salcombe Rd. Alf DE55 .... 5 B3
Samuel Ct. Ripley DE5 .... 16 B4
Sandbed La. Belper DE56 ..... 15 B2
Sandhall La. Spout DE56 .... 7 C3
Sandham La. Ripley DE5 .... 10 B1
Sandown Ave. Derby DE3 ..... 29 B2
Sandy La. Crich DE4 .... 8 C4
Sandy La. Hors DE21 .... 23 A2
Sandyford La. Alder DE56 ...... 7 C2
Sandyford La. Spout DE56 ...... 7 C2
Sarah Cl. Som DE55 .... 11 B4
Sawmills Ind Pk. Hean DE75 . 17 B2
Saxondale Ave. Derby DE3 ... 29 B2
Saxton Ave. Hean DE75 .... 17 C1
Scalby Cl. East NG16 .... 18 B1
Scargill Wlk. East NG16 .... 18 C2
Scarsdale Ave. Derby DE23 .. 28 B2
Scarsdale Rd. Duff DE56 ...... 21 C2
School Croft. Som DE55 .... 11 B3
School House Hill. Heage DE56
.... 9 B1
School La. Crich DE4 .... 3 A1
School La. Heage DE56 .... 9 B1
School La. Ripley DE5 .... 10 B1
Scothches The. Belper DE56 .. 14 C3
Scott Dr. Belper DE56 .... 15 C3
Scott Dr. Som DE55 .... 11 B4
Seaford Way. Ilk DE7 .... 25 C3
Seaton Cl. Derby DE3 .... 29 B2
Sedgefield Gn. Derby DE3 .... 29 B1
Sedgwick St. La Mill NG16 .... 18 A2
Sevenoaks Ave. Derby DE22 . 29 C3
Severn Sq. Alf DE55 .... 5 A2
Seymour Rd. East NG16 .... 18 C1
Shakespeare Dr. Alf DE55 ...... 5 A2
Shaw La. Belper DE56 .... 22 A4
Shaw La. Hollow DE4 .... 2 B4
Shaw Wood View. S Wing DE55 3 C2
Shaw St. Som DE55 .... 11 B3
Shaw's Yd. Kilb DE56 .... 22 C4
Shawcroft Ave. Som DE55 .... 11 B3
Shaws Hill. Crich DE4 .... 2 B1

Sheldon Rd. Hean DE75 .... **17** B3
Shelford Cl. Derby DE3 .... **29** B2
Shelford La. Hollow DE4 .... **2** A4
Shepton Cl. Ship DE7 .... **25** B2
Sherbourne Dr. Belper DE56 .. **15** B3
Sherwood Foresters Regiment
Meml. Crich DE4 .... **2** C2
Sherwood Rise. East NG16 .... **18** C1
Sherwood St. Som DE55 .... **11** B4
Shipley Ct. Ilk DE7 .... **25** B1
Shipley Ctry Pk. Ship DE75 .... **24** C3
Shipley Ctry Pk Visitor Ctr. Ship
DE75 .... **24** C4
Shipley La. Mapp DE75 .... **24** C3
Shipley La. Ship DE75 .... **24** C3
Shireoaks. Belper DE56 .... **14** B3
Shirley Rd. Ripley DE5 .... **10** B1
Shirley Rd. Swan DE55 .... **10** C4
Shop La. N Heage DE56 .... **9** B1
Short Ave. Derby DE22 .... **28** C3
Short Lands. Belper DE56 ...... **15** A2
Short Row. Belper DE56 .... **14** C2
Short St. Belper DE56 .... **15** A2
Shuckstone La. Crich DE4 .... **2** C3
Siddals La. Derby DE22 .... **28** C2
Sidney Cl. Derby DE3 .... **29** C2
Silver Birch Cres. Black DE55 . **5** B4
Silverhill Prim Sch. Derby DE3 ......
.... **29** B2
Simon Fields Cl. Stanl DE7 .... **24** A1
Sinclair Cl. Hean DE75 .... **24** B4
Sitch La. Callow DE4 .... **6** A2
Sitwell Dr. Kilb DE56 .... **23** A4
Skeavington's La. Ilk DE7 ...... **25** C3
Skiddaw Dr. Derby DE3 .... **29** C1
Skipton Cl. Ship DE7 .... **25** B2
Slack La. Derby DE22 .... **28** C1
Slack La. N Heage DE56 .... **9** B2
Slack La. Ripley DE5 .... **10** B1
Slack La. Ship DE75 .... **24** C4
Slack La. Som DE55 .... **11** B3
Slack La. Wess DE55 .... **3** B4
Slade La. W Und DE6 .... **26** C4
Slaidburn Cl. Derby DE3 .... **29** C1
Slater Cres. Wirk DE4 .... **6** C4
Sledgegate La. Hollow DE4 ..... **2** A4
Sleetmoor La. Som DE55 ...... **11** A4
Sleetmoor La. Swan DE55 ...... **11** A4
Smalley Mill Rd. Hors DE21 .. **23** A2
Smalley Mill Rd. Smal DE7 ... **23** A2
Smedley Ave. Som DE55 .... **5** B1
Smeeton St. Hean DE75 .... **18** A1
Smith Ave. Codnor DE5 .... **11** A1
Smith Dr. La Mill NG16 .... **18** A2
Smith-Hall La. H Ward DE6 ... **19** A4
Snake La. Duff DE56 .... **21** C2
Snowberry Ave. Belper DE56 . **15** A2
Snowdrop Valley. Crich DE4 .... **9** A4
Snowfield View. Wirk DE4 ...... **6** C3
Somercotes Hill. Som DE55 .. **11** B4
Somercotes Inf Sch. Som ....
.... **11** B4
Somerlea Park Jun Sch. Som ....
.... **11** B4
Somme Rd. Quar DE22 .... **28** A2
South East Derbyshire Coll. Hean
DE75 .... **17** C1
South Pl. Ripley DE5 .... **10** B1
South St. East NG16 .... **18** C1
South St. Som DE55 .... **11** B3
South St. Swan DE55 .... **10** C4
South Wingfield Prim Sch. S Wing
DE55 .... **3** C2
Southcroft. Alf DE55 .... **5** A2
Southgate Cl. Derby DE3 .... **29** B2
Southwood House Specl Sch. Holbr
DE56 .... **22** B3
Sovereign Way. Hean DE75 ... **17** B1
Spanker La. N Heage DE56 ...... **9** A1
Spanker Terr. N Heage DE56 ... **9** B1
Spencer Ave. Belper DE56 ... **15** A2
Spencer Dr. Som DE55 .... **11** B4
Spencer Rd. Belper DE56 ...... **15** A2
Spencer St. Stanl DE7 .... **24** A1

Spinners Way. Belper DE56 ... **15** B3
Spinney The. Belper DE56 ..... **15** A3
Spinney The. Ripley DE5 .... **10** B2
Spout La. Spout DE56 .... **7** B2
Spout La. Tans DE4 .... **1** A2
Spring Cl. Belper DE56 .... **14** C3
Spring Garden Terr. Ilk DE7 ... **25** C1
Spring Hollow. Haz DE56 ...... **21** B4
Spring La. Hean DE75 .... **17** C1
Spring Rd. Som DE55 .... **11** C3
Springdale Cl. Derby DE3 .... **29** C1
Springfield Ave. Hean DE75 ... **17** A3
Springfield Cl. Crich DE4 .... **3** A1
Springfield Cres. Som DE55 .. **11** B4
Springfield Dr. Duff DE56 ...... **21** B2
Springfield Gdn. Ilk DE7 .... **25** B2
Springfield Terr. Ripley DE5 .. **10** C1
Springfield View. Ripley DE5 . **10** B1
Springhill Way. Codnor DE5 .. **17** A4
Square The. Derby DE3 .... **29** B1
St Agnes Ave. Derby DE22 .... **28** B2
St Alkmund's Cl. Duff DE56 ... **21** C2
St Alkmunds Way. Duff DE56 . **21** C2
St Andrew's Dr. Swan DE55 ... **10** C4
St Andrews Cl. Swan DE55 .... **11** A4
St Benedict RC Sch. Derby ....
DE22 .... **28** C1
St Benet's Sch. Alder DE56 ..... **8** A4
St Edmund's Cl. Derby DE22 . **28** C2
St Elizabeth's RC Prim Sch. Belper
DE56 .... **14** C3
St George's Pl. Belper DE56 .. **14** C2
St Helen's La. Wirk DE56 .... **7** A4
St James Cl. Belper DE56 ...... **15** B2
St James' Dr. Brin NG16 .... **18** B4
St John's CE Prim Sch. Belper ....
DE56 .... **15** A3
St John's CE Prim Sch. Ripley ....
DE5 .... **10** C1
St John's Cl. Derby DE22 .... **28** B2
St John's Dr. Kilb DE56 .... **23** A4
St John's Rd. Belper DE56 ..... **15** A2
St John's Rd. Smal DE7 .... **23** C3
St John's St. Wirk DE4 .... **6** C4
St Johns Cl. Ripley DE5 .... **10** C1
St Lawrence Cl. Hean DE75 ... **17** C1
St Mary's Gate. Wirk DE4 .... **6** C4
St Matthew's Wlk. Derby DE22 ......
.... **28** C1
St Mawes Cl. Derby DE22 ..... **28** B2
St Mellion Cl. Derby DE3 ...... **29** C1
St Michael's Cl. Holbr DE56 .. **22** B3
St Michaels Cl. Crich DE4 .... **2** C1
St Nicholas Cl. Derby DE22 ... **28** B1
St Peter's Cl. Belper DE56 ..... **14** C2
St Peters Croft. Belper DE56 .. **15** A2
St Ronan's Ave. Duff DE56 .... **21** C1
Stable Cl. Hollow DE4 .... **2** A3
Stafford Cl. Smal DE7 .... **23** C3
Stafford Cres. Wirk DE4 .... **6** C4
Staines Cl. Derby DE3 .... **29** B1
Stainsbro' La. Callow DE4 .... **6** A3
Stainsbro' La. Cars DE4 .... **6** A3
Stainsby Ave. Hean DE75 ...... **24** C4
Stainsby Ave. H Wood DE7 ... **23** C3
Stamford Cl. Hean DE75 .... **17** C1
Stamford St. Ilk DE7 .... **25** C1
Stanage Gn. Derby DE3 .... **29** C1
Stanhope Rd. Derby DE3 .... **29** C2
Stanley Ave. Ripley DE5 .... **10** C1
Stanley Comm Prim Sch. Stanl .....
DE7 .... **24** A1
Stanley St. Som DE55 .... **11** B4
Stanstead Rd. Derby DE3 ...... **29** B2
Stanton Ave. Belper DE56 ..... **15** A2
Stapleton Rd. Ilk DE7 .... **25** C2
Starcross Ct. Derby DE3 .... **29** B2
Starthe Bank. Hean DE75 ...... **17** C1
Station App. Duff DE56 .... **21** C2
Station Ct. Ilk DE7 .... **25** C1
Station La. Codnor DE5 .... **17** A3
Station La. Iron NG16 .... **11** C2
Station Rd. Amber DE56 .... **8** C2
Station Rd. Denby DE5 .... **16** A2

Station Rd. Derby DE74 .... **29** B2
Station Rd. Duff DE56 .... **21** C2
Station Rd. Hean NG16 .... **18** A1
Station Rd. Ilk DE7 .... **25** C1
Station Rd. La Mill NG16 .... **18** A1
Staverton Dr. Derby DE3 .... **29** B2
Steam Mill La. Ripley DE5 ..... **17** A4
Stewart St. Som DE55 .... **11** B3
Stirland St. Codnor DE5 .... **11** A1
Stoddard Dr. Hean DE75 .... **17** C1
Stoke Cl. Belper DE56 .... **15** C3
Stoneleigh Way. Swan DE55 . **10** C4
Stoney La. Brin NG16 .... **18** B3
Stoney Wood Dr. Crich DE4 .... **2** B1
Stony La. Holbr DE56 .... **22** B3
Stoodley Pike Gdns. Derby ....
DE22 .... **28** B1
Stoppard Cl. Ilk DE7 .... **25** B1
Storer La. Spout DE56 .... **7** A2
Stranfaer Cl. Swan DE55 .... **11** A4
Stratford St. Ilk DE7 .... **25** C2
Street La. Denby DE5 .... **16** A3
Street La. Ripley DE5 .... **16** A3
Street Lane Prim Sch. Denby ....
DE5 .... **16** A1
Strelley Ave. Ripley DE5 .... **16** B4
Stretton Cl. Derby DE3 .... **29** B1
Strutt St. Belper DE56 .... **14** C2
Sudbury Mews. East NG16 ... **18** C1
Summer Dr. Wirk DE4 .... **6** C4
Summer La. Wirk DE4 .... **6** C4
Summerfields Way. Ship DE7 **25** B2
Summerfields Way S. Ilk DE7 **25** B1
Sun La. Crich DE4 .... **2** C1
Sunningdale Ave. Hean DE75 **24** C4
Sunny Bank Gdns. Belper ....
DE56 .... **14** C1
Sunny Hill. Belper DE56 .... **21** C4
Surgery La. Crich DE4 .... **3** A1
Sutton Ct. East NG16 .... **18** C1
Swanwick Hall Sch. Swan ....
DE55 .... **10** C4
Swanwick Hill. Swan DE55 ... **10** C4
Swanwick Prim Sch. Swan ....
DE55 .... **10** B3
Swanwick Rd. Som DE55 ...... **11** A4
Swayfield Cl. Derby DE3 .... **29** B2
Swift Ct. East NG16 .... **18** C1
Swinney Bank. Belper DE56 .. **15** A3
Swinney La. Belper DE56 ...... **15** A3
Sycamore Ave. Derby DE65 .. **29** B2
Sycamore Ave. Ripley DE5 .... **16** B4
Sycamore Cl. Mapp DE7 .... **24** C2
Sycamores The. East NG16 ... **18** C1
Sywell Cl. Swan DE55 .... **10** C4

Taghole La. W Und DE6 .... **19** C1
Tamar Ave. Derby DE22 .... **28** B2
Tamworth St. Duff DE56 .... **21** C2
Tamworth Terr. Duff DE56 ..... **21** C2
Tansley Ave. Stanl DE7 .... **24** A1
Tansley Prim Sch. Tans DE4 ... **1** A2
Tants Meadow. Hors DE56 .... **22** C3
Tantum Ave. Hean DE75 .... **17** B2
Taplow Cl. Derby DE3 .... **29** B1
Tasman Cl. Derby DE3 .... **29** C2
Tatham's La. Ilk DE7 .... **25** C1
Tavistock Ave. Ripley DE5 ..... **10** B1
Tavistock Sq. Alf DE55 .... **5** A3
Tawney Croft. Tans DE4 .... **1** A2
Tay Wlk. Derby DE22 .... **28** C2
Taylor La. Hean DE75 .... **17** B2
Taylor St. Ilk DE7 .... **25** C1
Taylor's La. Spout DE56 .... **7** A2
Telford Cl. Derby DE3 .... **29** C1
Tennyson St. Ilk DE7 .... **25** C2
Tenter La. Heage DE56 .... **9** B1
Thames Cl. Derby DE22 .... **29** C3
Thatchers La. Tans DE4 .... **1** A2
Thirlmere Ave. Derby DE22 ... **28** C2
Thistle Green Cl. Hean DE75 . **18** A1
Thompson St. La Mill NG16 ... **18** A2
Thomson Dr. Codnor DE5 ...... **17** A4

Thoresby Cl. Ripley DE5 .... **10** C1
Thorn Cl. Derby DE22 .... **28** B2
Thorn Tree Gdns. East NG16 . **18** C2
Thorpe Croft. Hollow DE4 .... **2** A3
Thorpe Dr. Derby DE3 .... **29** C2
Thorpe Hill Dr. Hean DE75 .... **24** C4
Thorpe Rd. East NG16 .... **18** C2
Thorpe St. Ilk DE7 .... **25** C2
Thorpe Way. Belper DE56 ..... **15** A3
Thorpe's Rd. Hean DE75 .... **17** B1
Thorpe's Rd. Ship DE75 .... **24** B4
Thorpelands Dr. Derby DE22 . **28** C1
Three Gates. Belper DE56 ..... **14** C1
Thurston Ave. Som DE55 ...... **11** B4
Ticknall La. Denby DE5 .... **16** A1
Tinkerley La. Idri DE6 .... **6** B1
Tinkerley La. K Ire DE56 .... **6** B1
Tinsley Rd. East NG16 .... **18** B1
Tiverton Cl. Derby DE3 .... **29** B2
Toadmoor La. Toad DE56 .... **8** C2
Top Farm Ct. Kilb DE56 .... **22** C4
Top Hagg La. Fritch DE56 .... **9** A3
Top La. Crich DE4 .... **2** B1
Top La. Shot DE56 .... **7** B1
Top Lons. K Ire DE56 .... **12** A4
Topshill La. K Ire DE6 .... **6** A1
Tor Ave. Som DE55 .... **11** B3
Tors The. Crich DE4 .... **2** C1
Tower Cl. Som DE55 .... **11** B4
Town St. Duff DE56 .... **21** C2
Town St. Holbr DE56 .... **22** B3
Towson Ave. La Mill NG16 .... **18** B1
Trent Gr. Alf DE55 .... **5** A1
Tresillian Cl. Derby DE22 ...... **28** C1
Trinity Cl. Ilk DE7 .... **25** C2
Trueman St. Ilk DE7 .... **25** C2
Tudor Falls. Hean DE75 .... **17** C2
Turnberry Cl. Ilk DE7 .... **25** B1
Turnditch CE Prim Sch. Turn ....
DE56 .... **13** A1
Turner Ave. La Mill NG16 ...... **18** A2
Turners La. Swan DE55 .... **11** A4
Turton Cl. La Mill NG16 .... **18** A2
Twyford Cl. Hean DE75 .... **24** B4

Uffa Magna. Derby DE3 .... **29** B1
Union St. S Norm DE55 .... **5** C3
Univ of Derby. Derby DE22 .... **28** B1
Upchurch Cl. Derby DE3 .... **29** B2
Upper Barn Cl. Hean DE75 .... **17** C1
Upper Dunstead Rd. Ald NG16 **18** A2
Upper Hall Cl. Holbr DE56 .... **22** B3
Upper Marehay Rd. Ripley ....
DE5 .... **16** B3
Upper Nelson St. Hean DE75 . **17** B1
Upton Cl. Hean DE75 .... **18** A1
Uttoxeter Rd. Derby DE65 ..... **29** C1

Vale The. Ilk DE7 .... **25** C2
Valley View. Belper DE56 ...... **15** A1
Valley View Dr. Stanl DE7 ..... **24** A1
Valley View Rd. Som DE55 .... **11** B2
Venture Cres. Som DE55 .... **5** A1
Vernon St. Ilk DE7 .... **25** C2
Vicarage Ave. Ilk DE7 .... **25** B2
Vicarage Cl. Belper DE56 ...... **15** A2
Vicarage Cl. Smal DE7 .... **23** C3
Vicarage Cl. Swan DE55 .... **10** C4
Vicarage Ct. Derby DE3 .... **29** B1
Vicarage Gdns. Hean DE75 ... **17** C1
Vicarage La. Duff DE56 .... **21** C2
Vicarage La. Iron NG16 .... **11** C2
Vicarage Mews. Som DE55 ... **11** C3
Vicarage Rd. Belper DE56 ..... **21** C4
Vicarage Rd. Derby DE73 ...... **29** B1
Vicarage St. Ilk DE7 .... **25** B2
Vicarwood Ave. Derby DE22 . **28** C1
Vicarwood Ave. Holbr DE56 .. **22** B4
Victoria Ave. Hean DE75 .... **17** B1
Victoria Cl. Derby DE3 .... **29** C2
Victoria Cotts. Som DE55 .... **5** B1
Victoria Cres. Iron NG16 .... **11** C2